TAUGHT BY
AMERICA

TAUGHT BY AMERICA

A STORY OF STRUGGLE
AND HOPE IN COMPTON

Sarah Sentilles

BEACON PRESS
BOSTON

Beacon Press
25 Beacon Street
Boston, Massachusetts 02108-2892
www.beacon.org

Beacon Press books
are published under the auspices of
the Unitarian Universalist Association of Congregations.

09 08 07 06   8 7 6 5 4 3 2 1

This book is printed on acid-free paper that meets the uncoated paper
ANSI/NISO specifications for permanence as revised in 1992.

Text design by Bob Kosturko
Composition by Wilsted & Taylor Publishing Services

Library of Congress Cataloging-in-Publication Data

Sentilles, Sarah.
Taught by America : a story of struggle and hope in Compton / Sarah Sentilles.
p.   cm.
Includes bibliographical references.
ISBN 0-8070-3273-5 (pbk. : acid-free paper)
1. Poor children—Education (Elementary)—California—Compton—Case studies.
2. Children of minorities—Education (Elementary)—California—Compton—Case studies.
3. Elementary school teachers—United States—Biography. 4. Teach for America
(Project)—Case studies. I. Title.
LC4093.S46 2005
372'.9794'94—dc22   2004028160

To ensure the privacy of my former students and their families, I have not
used their real names and have changed certain details that might identify them.
I have not changed the in-class and real-world experiences we shared.

For the students in Rooms 8 and 18.
And for my parents, who made this book possible.

Generations do not cease to be born, and we are responsible to them because we are the only witness they have. The sea rises, the light fails, lovers cling to each other, and children cling to us. The moment we cease to hold each other, the moment we break faith with one another, the sea engulfs us and the light goes out.

James Baldwin, *The Price of the Ticket*

CONTENTS

INTRODUCTION
A CLASS PICTURE

After I graduated from Yale in 1995 with a degree in literature,
I joined Teach for America (TFA), an organization that places
recent college graduates in underfunded, underresourced public schools where there are teacher shortages. I was placed in a
first grade classroom at Madison Elementary School in Compton, California. Compton is a city of ten square miles with a
population of about one hundred thousand in the heart of Los
Angeles. In the last thirty years, the city has shifted from being
predominantly white to black and then to Latino. Bordered on
the south by Long Beach and on the north by Watts, Compton
is in the area of Los Angeles often referred to as "South Central."[1] A twenty-one-year-old blond white woman from Texas
with almost no teaching experience, I was in charge of thirty-
six first graders, many whose first language was Spanish. My
classroom had no books. The ceiling was falling down.

My decision to apply for Teach for America was almost ac-
cidental. I had not planned to be a teacher. I actually planned
to pursue a doctorate in comparative literature. I thought it
might be a good idea to take time off between degrees, though,
so I visited Yale's career services to see what I could find. The
choices seemed to be investment banking or the Peace Corps.
TFA seemed a happy compromise between these two extremes,
a good, respectable thing to do as a break, and so I applied.

During my TFA interview, I was required to teach a five-minute lesson. My "students" were the other applicants. Wearing a new light green suit I had bought for all the job interviews I hoped to have during my senior year, I taught a lesson on the difference between similes and metaphors. After teaching my short lesson and sitting through six other lessons, I had a group interview and then a one-on-one interview. During that interview, I was handed a piece of paper on which were listed all of the possible sites where TFA places teachers. The interviewer asked me to check off where I would be willing to go. "The more flexible you are," he said, "the more likely it is that you will be accepted." I really wanted to stay on the East Coast, so I put a check mark by all the East Coast cities listed. At the last minute, for no clear reason, I checked off Los Angeles.

A month later I received a letter in the mail from TFA. I had been accepted, but I was not yet assigned to an area. I was told I would be notified in a month. I spent the next month anxiously regretting my last-minute choice of Los Angeles. When I could not wait any longer, I called TFA. "Please not LA," I thought to myself while the phone rang. "Please not LA."

A woman answered the phone. I could hear her shuffling through her files to find my information. "Sarah Sentilles," she said. "You have been placed in Los Angeles. Compton Unified School District.[2] Madison Elementary School."

I was devastated. Compton? Isn't that in South Central Los Angeles? Aren't there gangs there?

I hung up the phone and ran upstairs in my dorm to see my friend Maylen Dominguez. She was moving to New York City. "Los Angeles will be fun," she said. "Just imagine it. You can live near the beach and rollerblade every day." I tried to embrace Maylen's vision of such a sunny life. Deep down, though, I knew TFA was something I wanted to be able to say I had done, not something I actually wanted to do. Nevertheless, I signed the two-year contract. After graduation, I packed all my belongings in cardboard boxes, shipped them home to Dallas, got on a plane, and flew home. I began my journey toward Los Angeles, toward Compton, reluctantly.

Before Teach for America sent me off to teach the students in America's schools, it sent me to its Summer Institute in Houston. For six weeks, I taught summer school in a group supervised by a mentor teacher. There were four other new TFA teachers in my group, and we were in charge of six kindergarten students in one of Houston's public schools. Four teachers, one mentor, six kids, for a half-day of summer school. I remember spending most of my time working with my group to create one giant bulletin board for the unit we were going to teach on shapes.

Our mentor was a twenty-two-year-old woman with only one year of teaching experience. One hot July afternoon, she sat my group down to share the secret to good discipline in the classroom. She had a teddy bear on her lap. "You see this bear?" she asked. "This is Officer Bear."

We looked at her, looked at the bear, and nodded.

"All you need for good classroom management is this bear, a chair, and a telephone. The phone doesn't need to be plugged in or anything. You just want to have one."

We nodded again.

"If you ever have to leave the room for any reason, just put

Officer Bear in the chair, put the phone right next to him, and tell the kids the phone line goes directly to the police. Tell them Officer Bear can see them, and if they do anything wrong, he will call the police and have their parents put in jail. Tell them that, and I promise you won't have any discipline problems."

Armed with this kind of teaching advice, a cell phone for "emergencies," and a newly developed knack for creating beautiful bulletin boards, I drove with my sister Emily from Texas to California in the Jeep my parents had leased for me as a graduation present. I was supposed to start teaching at Madison Elementary School in Compton in two weeks. We listened to Coolio's song "I Remember" and sang the lyrics: "Compton, California, where the killers grow/Forced to lead a life that I didn't know."

"Sarah," Emily said, "did you hear that? Compton, California. That's where you're going."

We rewound the song and listened again.

"He didn't say 'Compton,' Emily. He said 'Come to California.'"

"No, Sarah, I think he really said 'Compton.'"

We listened again. He said "Compton."

We rewound the song. I sang loudly, "Compton, California, where the killers grow/Forced to lead a life that I didn't know." I finished the verse myself, "I'm Coolio!" We started laughing. And then I started crying. I told Emily about the dreams I had been having since I found out that I had been placed in Compton. Every night I dreamt I got shot. I felt the bullet break through my skin and leave a hole, a hot, numb, vacant spot.

"I'm afraid I am going to die," I told her.

• • •

When I first arrived in Los Angeles, I lived in Hollywood in a second-story apartment with a woman I knew from a summer program in college, Amy Levinson. She, too, was a TFA teacher in Compton, assigned to a middle school. I had always lived in dorms at Yale, and this was my first apartment. I had to learn how to pay bills, grocery shop, and cook. While I was learning to be an adult, I was also learning to be a teacher. Every day, for a year, I commuted from our apartment in Hollywood to Madison Elementary School in Compton where I taught first grade.

I immediately discovered that teaching was anything but time off. I was overwhelmed and exhausted every day. I woke up before 5:00 a.m. each school day, made myself breakfast and packed a lunch, drove to the nearest copy shop to make copies for that day's lesson, and then hightailed it to Compton. I taught thirty-six students all day, and then I cleaned my classroom, graded papers, planned the following day's lessons, drove home, opened a can of something to eat for dinner, and practically fell into bed. I often cried myself to sleep. The next morning it started all over again.

In October, a little over a month after I moved to Los Angeles and started teaching, my mom visited me for my twenty-second birthday. I bought us tickets to a play. On our way home from the play, we drove by a dead body lying in the middle of the highway. The traffic was thick, so we had to slow down. "Don't look, Sarah," she said.

The next morning she told me about a church in Pasadena. She had seen the rector of the church interviewed on a television program about the LA riots. She thought the name of the church was Christ Church, the name of the Episcopal church in which she grew up. We drove to Pasadena looking for Christ Church; we found All Saints instead.

The Sunday of our first visit to All Saints was a rock 'n' roll service, complete with electric guitars and drums. At the end of some of the songs, the entire congregation would break into applause, even whistling. I had never been in a church with electric guitars. I had never been in a church where people clapped and whistled. The place was alive, celebrating, hopeful. The sermon was incredible. I cried through the entire service, and I went back the next week, and the week after that, and the week after that. I felt like someone had glimpsed my soul and built a church around it. I went to church every Sunday desperate, needy, and afraid maybe this week's service would not fill me up the way last week's had. I didn't know how I would get up on Monday morning if it did not. In my mind, I carried my students with me to church. Sometimes I felt like I took up an entire pew.

All Saints was the first place in Los Angeles where people called me by my first name. I did not have to be Ms. Sentilles there. I got to be Sarah. No one wanted or needed anything from me. I had permission to weep. Sometimes I cried so hard during Sunday morning services that I had to go outside and sit on the stone steps leading into the church. I cried and rocked, cried and rocked. Strangers offered me tissues—gentle, kind gestures that often made me cry harder. Teaching in Compton forced me to take faith out of my head and move it into my heart, into my life. All Saints showed me how to do that.

At the end of my first school year, things at Madison were falling apart. The teachers hated the principal; the principal hated the teachers. In the middle of that disaster, I was recruited by the principal at another school in Compton, Garvey Elementary School, to come work with her. That principal, Mrs. Ramsey, was incredible—bright, committed, energetic, and supportive. The teachers at her school loved her, and they seemed to have books and clean classrooms, things missing from Madison. She promised me the supplies I needed to teach art and to create a school garden, and she recruited me along with several of the teachers I knew and respected at Madison. I was devastated to be leaving my Madison students, but I also felt like I was jumping from a sinking ship into a lifeboat. I longed to take my students with me, but I left Madison alone.

I spent the summer after my first year in Europe with my sister, a more than strange juxtaposition to my life in Compton. We traipsed around various countries, sharing one backpack between the two of us. At the end of the summer, I returned to Los Angeles to discover that the principal who had recruited me had been promoted to a position in the district offices and was no longer at Garvey. All the other teachers who had been recruited to teach at Garvey left as well. Their vacancies were filled by new TFA teachers, and her vacancy was filled by a principal who was possibly worse than the one I had fled at Madison. At that point, so close to the beginning of the school year, I had no choice but to teach second grade at Garvey. I also moved to an apartment in Venice Beach and lived with one of my best friends from Yale, Yuki Murata, who had recently moved to Los Angeles. Garvey was, really, no different than Madison. My new students were as loving and brilliant as my first students. My classroom still had no books. My days were just as long, my body just as exhausted, and my mind just as undone.

I can't honestly say I didn't know about poverty, racism, and injustice before I taught in Compton. I knew—I simply chose to ignore what I knew, an ignorance that was, in the words of author Ruth Ozeki, an act of will, "a choice one makes over and over again, especially when information overwhelms and knowledge has become synonymous with impotence."[3] After two years of teaching in Compton, however, such active ignorance was impossible. The surface of my world was shattered. My professor, theologian Elisabeth Schüssler Fiorenza, describes this kind of shattering—known in theoretical and political circles as conscientization—as a kind of conversion. Understanding shattering as conversion offers a choice: you can desperately try to put the pieces back together as they once were, or you can choose to make something new. In Compton, I was faced with this kind of conversion. I witnessed suffering, resilience, survival, joy, violence, love, and deep pain. I witnessed the workings of systemic oppression—oppression that had served my interests even as it remained invisible to me—and I knew I faced a choice: will I work against oppression or will I continue to benefit from it without trying to resist it? How must I respond? I responded by spending my third year in Los Angeles writing this book. I also responded by changing the course of my life. Instead of applying to doctoral programs in comparative literature, I applied to divinity schools, and I entered the ordination process in the Episcopal Church. I chose to make something new.

Although most of the action in this book took place almost ten years ago, not much has changed in the Compton schools. I wish this were not the case. I wish there were no need to tell these stories now.

The book unfolds in five chapters: "What I Did Not Know," "In My Classroom," "A Different Violence," "What We Need," and "A Kind of Belonging." Each chapter is a collection of stories, portraits of students and teachers. Through their stories a story of Compton will emerge, and so will my own. *Taught by America* is a window through which a different America can be seen, an America that, for some, has been hidden, an America that is, I believe, best seen through the stories of children. Glimpsing this America turned me inside out. I hope my writing will do for the reader what my experience in Compton did for me. And I hope, somehow, that it will make a difference.

CHAPTER I
WHAT I DID NOT KNOW

O N THE FIRST DAY I was required to be at Madison Elementary School, I drove there early in the morning. I turned onto Riverdale Avenue and drove slowly past the front of the school. A faded mural was painted across the top of the building. I could barely make out that it said "Madison Lions." I parked my car in the faculty parking lot, a small parking lot surrounded by a sagging chain link fence. Being allowed to park in the faculty parking lot, which was actually the only parking lot, made me giggle. I was still unused to thinking of myself as a teacher. Just three short months before I had been a college student. Maybe there will be a teachers' lounge, I thought.

I sat in the car for several minutes. I was not sure what to do or where to go. I decided to leave all the boxes of stuff I had bought for my classroom in the car and try to find the office. I walked from the parking lot through a long breezeway, classrooms on one side and beautiful rosebushes on the other. The building was in complete disrepair. Paint peeled from the walls, wooden boards covered windows, and the small patch of grass in front of the school desperately needed water. At the end of the breezeway, I found the office, a small room on my left. There was no sign telling me this was the office, but the door was open, and I could see what looked like a front desk. I walked in. The front desk was high, long, and narrow and served as a barrier between the front of the office and the back, where there was a copy machine and a door with a sign that read "Principal." No one was at the front desk.

"Hello?" I called out in the empty room. "Hello?" I was so nervous my voice cracked.

A woman appeared from the principal's office. "Hello," she said.

"I'm Sarah Sentilles, and I am going to be a first grade teacher here."

"OK," she said. "I'm Mrs. Gutierrez, and I am the school secretary. You're the first one here. Would you like your key?"

"My key?" I asked.

"The key to your classroom."

"Oh, of course, sure, thank you."

She reached underneath the front desk and brought up a brown rectangular board filled with keys hanging on small hooks. "I think you are in Room 8." She searched through the lines of keys, found the one for Room 8, and handed it to me. "At the end of the day you have to hang your key back on this board so we know who is here and who has gone home, in case there is an emergency."

"OK," I said. I did not know what to do next, so I just stood there and looked at her. She looked back at me. I could feel drips of sweat running down my legs.

"You can go to your classroom now," she said.

"OK," I said. "Thank you." I turned and walked out the door, but then I realized I had no idea where I was going. I went back inside.

"I'm sorry," I said, "but I don't know where Room 8 is."

"Your classroom is in the second row of buildings. I think it is the second room on the left. There are numbers on the doors."

"Thank you."

I walked out of the office past the first row of buildings to the second row. A strip of grass divided the two rows of classrooms. I walked past the first door, and then I came to a door marked with the number 8. There were three small holes in the middle of the door. I bent down to have a closer look. Bullet holes. I used my new key to open the door, and I walked into my classroom for the first time.

The poor condition of the room did nothing to quell my excitement. This room was mine. My own classroom. I am, at heart, a dork, a nerd, a goody two-shoes. I have always loved school. Late August, back to school time, is one of my favorite times of year. The promise of a fresh start always makes me giddy. When I was in grade school, my mother would pile me and my three siblings into our Suburban to go buy school supplies. Our school sent us a list of things we needed: binders, spiral notebooks, folders, pencils, pens, markers, crayons, rulers. I loved wandering the aisles at the office supply store, agonizing over what color binder or spiral to pick. When we got home, we would line up all our new supplies on the living room carpet so my dad could examine each item when he got home from work. Pink Pearl erasers were his favorite. Every year on the first day of school, my two sisters, my brother, and I would put on our new school clothes and line up on the driveway for a photograph. I was always so excited the night before going back to school that my stomach hurt.

I felt that kind of excitement standing in the doorway of

my new classroom. A pile of desks was in the middle of the room, some upright and some upside-down. A collection of small blue plastic chairs was stacked on a multicolored rectangular rug. I walked to the chalkboard. I could find no chalk and no erasers. The surface of the board was a disaster. Most of it was marred by water damage, and it looked like someone had tried to write on the wavy surface of the board with markers instead of chalk. One classroom wall was covered with three long bulletin boards. A sink and a low row of cupboards lined the back of the room. In one corner was a big metal desk.

I decided to get right to work putting the room together. First I swept. Then I righted the desks and arranged them in groups of six. I put the rug at the front of the room near the chalkboard. I made several trips to my car, lugging folders, pencils, markers, and paint to my classroom. I hung the laminated signs I had made, creating a science area by the sink, and designating one bulletin board for math work, one for language arts, and one for our calendar and job wheel. I stopped to look around the room. It was starting to look like a classroom. I sat down in one of the little blue chairs. I had no idea what to do next.

Just at that moment, Mrs. Gutierrez knocked on my door. "Excuse me, Ms. Sentilles," she said. "I thought you might like to have your class roster."

"Thank you," I said.

"It looks good in here," she said. She handed me a piece of paper with a long list of student's names—I counted thirty-six. At the top of the roster it said, "Room 8: Bilingual."

"This is the bilingual classroom?" I asked.

"Yes," she said. "You speak Spanish, right?"

"I try," I said. I had taken three years of Spanish in high school, and for my literature major at Yale, I'd been required to study literature written in a language other than English. I chose Spanish, but basically I faked my way through these classes. I bought the English translation of whatever book I was assigned, and, because the class was also taught in Spanish, I depended on my roommate Maylen, who took these classes with me and was fluent in Spanish, to help me figure out what was going on when I couldn't understand what the professor was saying.

"You're the only first grade teacher who speaks Spanish, so you'll get the students whose first language is Spanish," Mrs. Gutierrez said.

"Don't a lot of students in Compton speak Spanish?" I asked.

"Yes," she said. "But our teachers don't."

When Mrs. Gutierrez left the room, I hugged the class roster to my chest. My students, I thought to myself. Mine. I started reading the list over and over. I tried to imagine that soon these names would be connected to real first graders who would line up every morning to come into my classroom. I opened the cellophane wrapped boxes of folders I had bought. I took out a Sharpie and started labeling folders with students' names. When I finished that, I wrote their names on the apple-shaped name tags I had made. Then I wrote their names on nameplates for their desks. Then I wrote their names on clothespins that we would use for the job wheel each week. I was deep in meditation. I felt connected to children I did not yet even know.

When I finished, I looked with satisfaction at the piles of labeled objects stacked all over the room. I took a deep breath, and then I panicked. I felt like I might throw up. Thirty-six children? I frantically started counting things. Desks: thirty. Chairs: thirty. Coat hooks: twelve. What was I going to do? My panic went deeper than numbers. Even if I had had enough seating for thirty-six students, I really had no idea what to do when I had thirty-six students in their seats.

The next day, Mrs. Gutierrez handed me a new roster when I picked up my key from the office. I quickly glanced at the names. "These names are different than the ones listed yesterday," I said.

"The roster will keep changing," she said. "Teachers joke around here that if you compare your original roster to the roster you have at the end of the year, over half of the names will be different."

I thought of the hours of labeling I had done the day before. "Oh," I said. "Thanks."

The changing roster was the first of many experiences in Compton in which I realized I really didn't know what I thought I knew. From the first moment of my first day of school, my greenness was obvious. Sometimes my inexperience was relatively harmless, resulting in botched lessons or an inability to get everything done that I needed to do. Other times my newness had more dangerous consequences—I bungled home visits, didn't contact Child Protective Services when I should have, and sometimes even failed to keep my students safe. While I was working in Compton, none of my assumptions held—not about who would be in my classroom each day, or how things were in the world, or who I was, or why I was in Compton, or what I would do when I was finished teaching. In the following pages are stories that illuminate moments when I could almost feel my brain changing, flipping over in my head, expanding—moments that took my breath away. Each story reveals me—a new, white teacher in Compton bumping up against the limits of my knowing and struggling to figure out what was required of me.

For the first month of school I had to remind myself that I was the teacher, that it was OK to park in the faculty parking lot, that the teachers' lounge (there really was one) was a place I was allowed to go, that the other members of the faculty were my colleagues. I usually felt more like a student. Although I was officially the teacher in Room 8, although I was the person who taught my students how to read, how to add and subtract, how to sit in chairs at desks, and how to paint, my students were really my teachers. When people discover I taught in Compton, they say, "Wow, that's a rough area," or "That must have been hard." Secretly, I enjoy the way people—and it is always white people—look at me like I did something courageous, but deep down, I know their assumptions are all wrong. Yes, teaching in Compton was hard, but what was even harder was learning in Compton. My own learning is what required courage.

✎ ✎ ✎

On the first day of school at Madison Elementary School, the custodian, Mr. Apple, was still moving desks into my room so every student would have a place to sit. When he brought the last one, an extra desk from the fifth grade much too tall for a first grader, it was time for morning recess. I walked my long line of thirty-six first grade students to the yard and let them go. As I watched them run to the playground, apple-shaped name tags (precariously attached to strings around their necks) flying, I realized I had not told them what to do at the end of recess. I had not told them where to line up or where to find me. I did not even know if there was a bell to signal the end of recess. I was gripped by the terror that I would never find my students again.

I didn't have to worry, though. At the sound of the bell signaling the end of recess, my students found me. Malcolm Daniels was the first student who returned. I was so relieved I almost hugged him.

"Do you think the other students will be able to find me?" I asked.

"Yes," he said. "Don't worry."

I soon discovered that Malcolm liked to be close to me. Whether I was teaching, watching my students at recess, or talking to another teacher, he would lean against me, holding the edge of my skirt or dress. His head came to just below my elbow, and I liked to lay my hand on his head while I talked to the rest of the class. His hair was cut very short, with shaved, curvy designs starting from his part and moving to the back of his head. Malcolm wrapped his arms around my waist and hugged me, hard, several times a day.

When I look at the photograph of my first grade class, I can find Malcolm easily. His smile takes up almost half his face. In the picture he is standing in the back row of bleachers, wearing a bright purple shirt. Purple was his favorite color, and I remember how excited he was to be wearing an outfit that was completely purple—purple shirt, purple shorts, purple socks. In the photo, he is doing exactly what we were instructed to do by the photographer. His hands are clasped tightly behind his back, he is looking at the camera, and he is smiling. When I look at this photograph, I am always struck by how small Malcolm was because he seemed to take up so much space in the classroom.

Malcolm could not read. He could not sit still in his seat for more than thirty seconds. But he could write the letter M. And he knew it was the first letter of his name. So he wrote it everywhere. Name: M. 2 + 2 = M. This M was the product of a long year of work in kindergarten by Malcolm and his teacher. They were both very proud of his progress.

The first art lesson I ever taught was a disaster. We were going to create construction paper gardens. I gave every student a big piece of blue construction paper, about twenty small squares of colored construction paper I had stayed up most of the night cutting, scissors, a bottle of glue, and stencils of leaves, stems, and petals. I delivered the supplies, and the second the last piece of paper was out of my hand, I realized what a stupid thing I had done. I watched my students looking at the big pile of supplies on their desks. I had not shown them what to do. In teacher talk, I had not "modeled" what to do, although that was a term I hadn't learned yet. I should have had them watch me create my own construction paper garden. I should have traced the flower parts, cut them, and glued them. I thought verbal instructions were enough, but first grade students need to hear what they are supposed to do, watch what they are supposed to do, and then do what they are supposed to do. Instead I simply said, "OK, let's make paper gardens." There was a flurry of tracing and cutting. Too late now. I just had to let them work.

About twenty minutes later, Malcolm finished his garden. At least he told me he had. He didn't show it to me, and I didn't ask to see it. He asked me if he could start to straighten the room. Malcolm loved to clean. Every day, he organized the library, swept every piece of paper from the floor, stacked books, straightened desks and chairs. When he got frustrated with a lesson, he would get up and begin to clean a section of the room. I always let him. I didn't know how to reach him, nor how to get him to sit still. I didn't know how to teach him to read, nor how to move him past the letter *m*. So I let Malcolm clean the room. It was a relief to have him occupied and quiet. I couldn't meet his needs, and often I didn't try.

So Malcolm started to clean. The room was a mess; tiny pieces of construction paper covered the floor. I reminded him to throw away just the scraps and to ask each student before he threw away anything that might be part of a garden. Malcolm nodded his head, picked up the trash can, and got to work.

After Malcolm had been cleaning for about ten minutes, one of the other students screamed. Malcolm, it seemed, had thrown away one of my student's carefully stacked pile of flower parts. Thirty minutes' worth of work cutting leaves, stems, and petals had been crumpled and dumped in the trash can. In fact

Malcolm, I soon discovered, had thrown away not just one student's stack, but all of the stacks. Several students started to cry. So did Malcolm.

I didn't know what to do, so I said, "Great. Good, Malcolm. Thank you for ending that project for us."

Malcolm looked at me. He was not sure if I was being serious or sarcastic. I was not sure either. Then I decided he really had helped us; the garden project was a disaster and belonged in the trash. I asked for a volunteer to help Malcolm collect the scissors and the glue and moved the class to the carpet so we could read a story together.

During the first quarter of school, I had to miss a day of school to attend a workshop about teaching math. I was worried about leaving my class with a substitute. I left the substitute a long letter and a detailed lesson plan. The letter began: "Welcome to Room 8! This is a very special class. Please take care of them for me and assure them I will return tomorrow." I loved my class, and I did not think they would be able to survive for a whole day without me. I believed I was essential, as if I could control what happened inside and outside my classroom, as if my presence kept my students safe.

I returned the next day, and before I even reached the classroom door, one of the girls in my class, Carmen Lopez, ran up to me and said, "Malcolm and his dad came to say good-bye yesterday. They are moving away. Malcolm is not going to be in our class anymore."

Just like that. He was gone. And I had missed the chance to say good-bye.

In Compton, students changed schools all the time. Parents moved or students were placed in different homes or they were switched to different classrooms. But Malcolm was the first student I lost. I didn't expect it. And it hurt.

Malcolm was the first student I lost. Taniqua Cameron was the second. Taniqua and her cousin Ranisha were both in my class. They looked more like sisters than cousins, but their similarities made their differences obvious. Ranisha seemed to be a cleaner, brighter, happier version of Taniqua. Ranisha came to school smiling, wearing brightly colored dresses with barrettes and hair rubber bands to match. Taniqua arrived quietly, hiding behind her school bag, her hair pulled back into a single ponytail. She rarely smiled.

In the middle of October, Ranisha was transferred to a different classroom, a common event in the Compton Unified School District. Throughout the school year, students were transferred from one classroom to another, sometimes even from one school to another, without notice and for no clear reason. Some students, like Malcolm, left the district by choice. Others were moved when administrators discovered halfway through the year that they were supposed to be learning to read in Spanish and had been placed in English-only classrooms. Several times I lost students who had been in my class for months for " number-balancing" reasons, and the very next day, a new student would arrive at my door holding on to his mother, who was clutching a small piece of blue paper stating that he was to be enrolled in my room.

After Ranisha was switched to a different class, I would find Taniqua and Ranisha leaning against the wall next to the water fountain clinging to each other and crying, every morning. I would hug them, separate them, and take them to their classrooms. Then Taniqua began to miss school two or three times a week. When I asked Ranisha where her cousin was, she would say, "She's sick."

"Again?" I always asked. Ranisha would just shrug her shoulders.

After several weeks of this, I asked the school nurse, Mrs. Jeffries, what I should do. Mrs. Jeffries was one of the few people at Madison Elementary School I trusted. She suggested I file a truancy report with Child Protective Services (CPS). Her suggestion terrified me. What would happen if I filed a truancy report and CPS took Taniqua away from her mother? What would happen if CPS came to Taniqua's house and told her mother I had filed a report against her and she got angry with me? I didn't want to be responsible for breaking up a family or getting outsiders involved in other people's business or jumping to conclusions about something I knew nothing about. But I was worried about Taniqua.

I decided not to file the truancy report.

A few days later, as I was pulling out of the driveway after school, I saw Taniqua and her brother playing ball in the street one block from school. Taniqua had been absent that day, so I stopped in the middle of the street, got out of my car, and said,

"Taniqua, what are you doing playing outside when you didn't come to school today?"

As I asked her this question, she seemed to shrink, to slink back and into herself. The smile she had while playing ball with her brother was gone. As I walked toward her, her brother ran to their house, shouting, "Mama, Mama, Taney's teacher's here and wants to know why Taney's playing outside when she didn't come to school."

I followed him to the front door. The outside door was made of a thick white metal covered with tiny holes allowing the person on the inside to see out and preventing the person on the outside from seeing in. I could not see Taniqua's mother, but I heard her say, "You tell that teacher my daughter can play outside and not go to school anytime I want her to."

I knocked on the front door.

Taniqua's mother opened the door and looked at me. She crossed her arms in front of her and continued to stare at me. I was nervous and a little bit scared. But I was also angry that she was keeping her daughter home from first grade. Taniqua was behind in every subject, especially reading.

"Hi, I'm Taniqua's teacher, Sarah Sentilles," I said.

"Yeah?"

"I was wondering why Taniqua has not been coming to school."

"She's been sick."

"Every day for two weeks?"

"Yeah."

"That's too bad. What's wrong with her?"

"Sore throat."

"Have you taken her to see a doctor?"

"Yeah."

"Well, she's really falling behind her classmates. It's important that she come to school every day."

"OK."

"Please send a doctor's note with her if she has to be absent again."

"OK," she said and closed the door. That was the end of our conversation.

I turned and walked to my car. From Taniqua's front walk I could see Madison Elementary School. Taniqua spent her days in a house one short block away from school. I could probably see her front door from my classroom. On my way to the car I stopped and hugged Taniqua. "Try to come to school, Taniqua. We really miss you."

She just stared at me. She looked like she was about to cry.

Taniqua came to school every day for the next two weeks. At the end of every school day, I would make her promise she would come back the next day. I would put my hands on her shoulders and look into her eyes and say, "Please come to school tomorrow. Tell your mom how important it is for you to come to school." In retrospect I regret that. I don't think it was a good idea for me to place the burden of going to school on a six-year-old. I don't think Taniqua had much control over her attendance. I think I made her feel bad about something that was not her fault.

After two weeks of perfect attendance, Taniqua's absences started again. This time, I filed the truancy report. Ten days later, I received a copy of the report in my mailbox at school.

On the bottom of the pink carbon copy was scrawled: "Visited home. Spoke to aunt." That was it.

After that, Taniqua came to school a couple of days each week. Then one day she stopped coming to school altogether, and I never saw her again.

❧ ❧ ❧

"Table four?"

"Table four?" I asked again, louder this time. "Table four, what are you doing?" Five of the students at the table were standing around Julio Gutierrez, mesmerized. I walked toward them.

"What's going on over here?" I asked. "You're supposed to be finishing your art project." We were studying habitats, and we had just read Eric Carle's *House for a Hermit Crab*. They were supposed to be working as a group to finish their addition to the giant hermit crab shell we were making.

"Julio's showing us how to throw our voices," Carmen said.

"What?" I asked.

Julio turned his bright eyes on me. "I'm showing them what it means to be able to throw your voice, you know, to be able to make it sound like someone else's voice, or to be able to make it sound like it is coming from another part of the room."

"Oh," I said. "Can you throw your voice, Julio?"

"Of course." He scooted his body toward the edge of his chair. He put both legs off to one side and began to kick them together, like the tail of a mermaid. He moved his arms like he was swimming the breaststroke under water. He cleared his throat. He started singing the theme from *The Little Mermaid*.

"Ah-ah-ah-ah-ah-ah-ah-ah." He was actually quite good.

Julio was obsessed with mermaids. He sang about them, drew them, painted them, and wrote about them at every opportunity. He could even construct mermaids out of the multi-colored, multishaped blocks we used in math. How he was able to build beautiful mermaids with trapezoids, hexagons, squares, and triangles still eludes me. The other students loved his mermaids, and they would often ask Julio to draw a mermaid on their work. Notwithstanding the fact that the mermaids were usually obviously out of place—showing up in students' drawings lounging in forests, sprawled on sidewalks in front of a house, or sitting at attention in a classroom—they were drawn with a skill that far exceeded the ability of most of the other students in the class. I tried to create an atmosphere where students believed the best artwork was their own artwork, not a copy of someone else's. Julio and I made a deal that he could draw as many mermaids as he desired, but he could draw them only on his own work. The sheer desire to draw mermaids, however, sometimes got the better of him. I would look at a student's work, see a beautifully drawn mermaid, and then glance at Julio, who would have been watching me the whole time. "Sorry," he would mouth.

In October, Julio's mother, Mrs. Gutierrez, the secretary at Madison Elementary School, had him switched out of the class to which he'd been assigned and into my classroom. "I think you're the best first grade teacher here," Mrs. Gutierrez whispered to me one morning. "I like the way your room looks. I like the kind of homework you send home. I like the way you interact with your students. I think good stuff is going on in your room."

Did she know I was just starting my second month of teaching? Her decision to move Julio into my room pleased but also terrified me. Would the other teachers hate me? Would his original teacher think I had done something to convince Mrs. Gutierrez to switch him? Would Mrs. Gutierrez be disappointed when she learned what really went on in my room?

Parents who came to Madison during the school day were often yelling. Parental frustration with the school district was high. Often parents yelled about overcrowded classrooms, inexperienced teachers, and inadequate school infrastructure, but sometimes they simply yelled about situations they might actually be able to remedy, like something that had been lost—a sweatshirt, a T-shirt, blue uniform pants, a pencil case, a book bag. I had more than one student cry when their new shoes got dirty. They thought they would get in trouble when they arrived home. It was impossible to keep shoes clean at Madison. The whole school was one giant patch of dry, dusty gravel that blew everywhere. Teaching at Madison was like walking on a beach in shoes and socks. When I got home at the end of a day of teaching, I had to take off my shoes and empty sand into the trash can.

Although our school had a sign proclaiming "Parents Welcome Here," the school seemed to do whatever possible to disempower and frustrate parents. Mrs. Gutierrez, however, knew how to negotiate the school system. Since she worked at the school her son attended, she knew the teachers, knew the principal, knew the people working at the district level. Like any parent, she wanted the best for her child. Mrs. Gutierrez chose me. What do you do when the best you can get for your son is a twenty-one-year-old white woman with no teaching experience and a classroom filled with thirty-six children?

Julio was clearly on a different level than the other students in my first grade classroom. He was an excellent reader, his handwriting was perfect, and he could write entire paragraphs. Some of the students in my room had never been to school before. By the time I reached first grade, I had been in school for three years—two years of preschool and one year of kindergarten. For many of my students, the first day of first grade was their first day of school. Ever. I had to teach them how to be in a classroom, how to hold a pencil, turn the pages of a book, sit at a desk, sit on the carpet—not to mention the things first graders are supposed to learn like reading and writing.

In the middle of the year, Julio's mother and I decided it would be a good idea to have him tested for Compton's gifted and talented program, GATE. She made an appointment to have Julio tested. When the day of his appointment arrived, she took a day off from working in the front office and took Julio to the district offices.

She came back in the afternoon looking very disappointed.

"How did it go?" I asked.

"Not well," she said.

"How do you know?" I asked, surprised.

"They asked him strange questions, Ms. Sentilles," she said, slowly shaking her head.

"Like what?"

"They asked him where hamburger comes from."

"What did he say?"

"The grocery store."

"That seems right to me," I said. "I think I would have said the same thing."

"Well, apparently the correct answer is that hamburger comes from a cow."

Many students in Compton had never been outside their city. When I took my students on field trips, they often pointed to the cement sides of the highway, slanted like hills, and said "Mountains!" Many had never even been to the beach. How would Julio know hamburger comes from a cow? Hamburger, in his life, came from the grocery store.

"I'm sorry," I said.

"It's okay," she said. "I like him being in your class. I think he's learning a lot." She reached across the office counter and rested her hand on my arm. "It will be fine," she said. "Don't you worry."

But there was so much to worry about.

One day in February, Carmen Lopez, one of the better read-ers in my class, stopped reading. Carmen was the main translator in my classroom. She was fluent in both Spanish and English, and she helped me make sure the students who were just learning English had a grasp on what was happening in the classroom. Suddenly, she no longer knew how to read. She sat at the table, staring at the page.

"I can't do it, Ms. Sentilles," she said. "It doesn't make sense to me anymore."

"What do you mean?" I asked.

"I think I don't know how to read anymore."

"Carmen, you know how to read. What's going on?"

"I don't know, Ms. Sentilles. I can't remember what I'm supposed to do."

It was as if Carmen had suddenly forgotten what letters meant, how to put sounds together into words, how to put words into sentences, how to tell a story. I called her mother; she came to meet with me after school. When I asked if there was anything going on at home that I should know about, she told me that she and Carmen's father were getting divorced.

"Carmen is very upset," she said.

"It seems like she has forgotten how to read," I said. Her mother nodded.

Carmen never again read as well as she had at the beginning of the year, and I don't really know what happened. I was confused. I wondered if I had imagined that she could read before, or if I was imagining now that she couldn't. But the evidence was there. Not only had Carmen's reading skills changed, so had her handwriting and the kind of artwork she created. Sometimes I sat and looked through the portfolio of her work I had collected throughout the year. The change was sudden and startling. Instead of the complete sentences she could write at the beginning of the year, she now wrote the same word over and over again. Often, this word was my name.

✎ ✎ ✎

Because Carmen was fluent in both English and Spanish, I asked her to sit next to Maria Garcia. Maria was silent for most of her time in my first grade classroom. She didn't speak English, and she couldn't read or write in Spanish. She was transferred into my class late in the school year. Maria had long, dark hair and a smile that came easily but quickly passed. Her eyes were quick; they didn't stay anywhere long, but darted around the room, never resting. Maria's right foot and ankle were covered by a huge burn scar—the stretched skin wavy, like patterns on a sandbar at the beach.

I first saw the scar after my roommate from college, Maylen, visited my classroom. Maylen spoke Spanish fluently, and Maria took to her immediately. While Maylen was helping the students at Maria's table, Carmen told Maria to show Maylen her scar. When she saw Maria's scarred foot, Maylen asked her what had happened. Maria said her mother had thrown hot beans on her foot. Carmen then told Maylen that Maria's twin sister's foot was scarred, too.

Maylen stood up from the table and walked to where I was working with some other students. "Sarah," she whispered, "Have you seen Maria's foot?"

"No," I said. "Why?"

"She has a huge scar and says her mother threw hot beans on her foot. She won't say anything else about it, though."

"Oh," I said, shrugging my shoulders as I turned back to continue reading with my students.

After lunch, I asked Maria to show me her foot. Then I taught my first graders a lesson on music and emotions. They listened to different kinds of music—classical, rock, rap—and drew whatever they thought best captured the feeling of the music. I watched Maylen as she drew with Maria.

That night I cried myself to sleep.

The next morning, I remembered another day at school when Maria had cut her hand by accident with a piece of paper. She didn't show anyone the cut, but kept her hand tightly clenched in a fist. I saw blood dripping down her arm. I asked her what had happened, and she opened her hand. It was covered in blood.

That same day I reported what I had seen on Maria's foot to the school nurse, Mrs. Jeffries. I told her I suspected child abuse. Mrs. Jeffries came to my classroom, pulled Maria to the back of the room, and asked her, in English, what had happened to her foot. I translated Mrs. Jeffries's questions into Spanish for Maria. She would not answer. She was silent, smiling her quiet smile.

Mrs. Jeffries turned to me and told me there was nothing we could do. She agreed the burn was suspicious, especially because both sisters had similar burns on their feet. "But," Mrs. Jeffries told me as she gently held Maria's scarred foot in her hand, "there is really nothing we can do about old wounds. If they are already healed, we cannot prove anything."

I asked Mrs. Jeffries to speak with Maria's mother after

school that day. Mrs. Jeffries agreed. I kept Maria in my room at the end of the day so her mother would have to come to my room to get her when Maria wasn't at the gate with the rest of our class. When Maria's mother came to the room to get Maria, Mrs. Jeffries was waiting there with me.

Mrs. Jeffries asked her questions in English, which I translated into Spanish. "We noticed the scars on your daughters' feet, and we wanted to know what happened," Mrs. Jeffries said.

Mrs. Garcia answered, "Una cosa de agua caliente se cayó."

"A pot of hot water fell on her foot," I told Mrs. Jeffries.

"What?"

"Qué?"

"Cuando ella y su hermana estaban jugando, ellas corrieron cerca de la estofa y pusieron los pies en algo caliente."

I translated for Mrs. Jeffries: "They were playing near the stove and running and the girls stepped in a hot pot." As I translated, I felt I was not understanding everything. What if I was not saying the right words?

Mrs. Jeffries looked at me and asked, "They stepped in a hot pot? Ask her what was in the pot."

Mrs. Garcia answered my question. "Agua caliente," she said.

"Hot water," I said. Then I added, "But that is not what Maria told me." While the three of us were talking, Mrs. Garcia pushed a stroller back and forth, back and forth. Inside the stroller was a tiny baby, sleeping, wrapped in pink blankets.

"Thank you for talking with us, Señora," Mrs. Jeffries said.

"Gracias por hablando con nosotros," I said. Mrs. Garcia didn't say anything more, and she didn't look at me. She simply turned and walked away, pushing the stroller ahead of her. Her twin girls followed her. Before they disappeared around the corner of the building, Maria turned around, saw me watching them, and waved.

🖋 🖋 🖋

Marco Quezada looked up from his desk and waved me over. We were in the middle of a lesson on estimation, one of the objectives in the state-mandated curriculum. I had designed a lesson on teeth. My first grade students were supposed to estimate the number of teeth they thought they had, have a friend count how many they actually did have, and then calculate the difference between what they had estimated and what they had in their mouths. I liked to combine art lessons and math lessons, so when they finished the "math" part and I had checked their work, they got to create their mouths on big pieces of black paper using chalk and tin foil. I explained the project, and my students got right to work.

Less than five minutes into the project, Marco waved to get my attention. While he waited for me, he sat quietly at his desk with his hands folded. "How are you doing, Marco?" I asked.

"I'm finished," he said.

"There is no way you have finished," I said. "Let me see your work."

He handed me his paper. For "estimated number of teeth" he had written "3." For "actual number of teeth" he had written "3." For "difference between estimated and actual number of teeth" he had written "0."

"Now, Marco," I said, "that is not funny. Let's get to work here. Estimate the number of teeth you think you have, and then ask someone to count them."

"I did," he said.

"No, you didn't. No one has three teeth."

"I do," he said.

I sighed, exasperated. I thought he was trying to be funny. Then he opened his mouth. I looked inside. I counted. One. Two. Three.

"I guess you do," I said. "Good job."

It had never occurred to me that a seven-year-old could have teeth so rotten that they had all fallen out. Moments like my experience with Marco happened every day, moments when my framework for understanding the world no longer worked, moments when I realized just how much I didn't know.

CHAPTER II
IN MY CLASSROOM

PUBLIC ELEMENTARY SCHOOL classrooms in Compton are self-contained—that is, one teacher in one classroom teaches every single subject to her students. I taught language arts, math, art, science, and physical education (lots of hokey pokey, head-shoulders-knees-and-toes, and steal the eraser). From 7:45 in the morning until 2:15, I was in charge of everything that thirty-six students learned.

I soon understood the importance of routine, both for me and for my students. From 7:45 until 8:00, we did "calendar math." We documented the day's weather (usually sunny in Southern California), and we puzzled out "Amazing Equations" using the numbers from that day's date. From 8:00 until 10:30, we rotated through language arts centers. The students were divided into homogeneous groups (this was a state mandate). Each group rotated through six centers. At one center, students met with me at a round table for reading instruction. At another center, students might lounge in our class library for free reading time. In another center, they might work on writing their own book. In another center, they might use handheld mirrors to create self-portraits and then write five sentences to describe themselves. The center activities, except for reading with me, changed every day. I was especially proud of the way I taught the students to rotate from one center to the next. Each group cleaned up at whichever center it was working. We all stood at the same time, lined up behind a strip of tape I had placed on the floor near each center, and walked, in silence, in a clockwise direction, to the next activity. It was, for me, a beautiful thing to observe.

For the last half hour of the language arts component, from 10:00 to 10:30, we all worked together. Sometimes I read a story on the rug, and we did an activity based on the book. Other times we did an activity based on the parts of speech. I put a giant piece of butcher paper on the board and divided it, using markers, into columns: adjectives, nouns, adverbs, verbs, prepositional phrases. Then we brainstormed words for each part of speech. Adjectives: furry, clean, smart, funny, green, fast, mean. Nouns: children, students, lizards, bears, chairs, dinosaurs. Verbs: laugh, skip, read, run, eat, jump. Adverbs: sleepily, quickly, magically, suddenly. Prepositional phrases: in a classroom, under a tree, in the bed, over a hill, to the store. Then, using the parts of speech, each student created sentences and illustrated them. For example: "Furry lizards run quickly to the store" or "Smart children skip sleepily under a tree."

From 10:30 to 10:45, we had morning recess. From 10:45 to 11:30 we did math. I liked group problem solving. I would pose a word problem to the class. They would work on the problem with their table groups, and then students would volunteer to show the class how they had chosen to solve the problem. I taped several pieces of butcher paper to the board, and one by one students came up to share their work. The more different ways that we could discover to solve the problem, the better. When they worked at the board, they got to use the scented markers I had in the room, so this was a favorite activity. From 11:30 to 12:15, we had lunch and recess. From 12:15 to 12:30, I read a story. From 12:30 to 1:00, we completed a group math activity. And from 1:00 to 2:00 we got to do art. I loved art history. Our art activities often involved studying a famous artist and then creating art inspired by that artist. We produced cubist paintings using sponges cut into squares and dipped in paint. We fashioned Miró-inspired mobiles. We made collages influenced by Jacob Lawrence. Science was not my strong suit as a teacher, so I tried to integrate it into other activities whenever I could—language arts lessons on habitat, measuring activities in which we made cookies, units on dinosaurs, math activities about the planets, experiments with water (which we then used for watercoloring). We also planted a garden. Near the end of the school day, at 2:00, we cleaned up, lined up, and walked to the gate to be met by parents, siblings, grandparents, and guardians.

Almost all of my teaching was based on instinct. I had had only six weeks of formal teacher training. I needed help. I desperately wanted help, but I also desperately wanted approval. When I arrived in Los Angeles, TFA connected me with a mentor, a retired teacher who would visit my classroom, observe me teaching, and share her expertise developed during years in the classroom. My mentor, a kind older white woman, came to my classroom a couple times. Although I wanted criticism, the perfectionist overachiever in me, driven by arrogance and pride, resisted showing anyone the places I might be less than perfect. My mentor told me when she would visit, and so I prepared. I designed the best lessons I knew how to design, I prepped my kids, and I cleaned my room like a mad woman. She believed she was observing a regular day in my classroom, but in some ways, she was watching a play.

Nevertheless, my failings were, I am sure, obvious. At the end of her first visit, we sat down together at one of the groups of student desks. She had pages of notes. I yearned for help, advice, concrete suggestions.

"Well, Sarah," she began. "It's a little loud in your room."

"Oh," I said. "I guess it is."

"I have an excellent suggestion for you."

"Great," I said.

"I think you need to wear softer shoes."

"Excuse me?"

"Your shoes make an awful lot of noise when you walk around. I recommend wearing shoes with rubber soles."

"OK."

"And I also noticed that you used incorrect grammar."

I was quiet.

"You said 'these ones' a few times, and that is simply not good English."

I thanked her for her time. I even wrote a thank you note.

This was the kind of advice I got during my entire time teaching in Compton. One experienced teacher at Madison told me to wear a slip. Another teacher suggested I cut slits in tennis balls and place one on the bottom of each leg of each chair in the room to make the room quieter.

I was required to turn in my lesson plan book at the beginning of every week, a spiral notebook filled with squares standing for each hour of the day. I diligently wrote my lessons in small, perfect, color-coded writing in each square, complete with objectives. The book would be returned to me the next day with the principal's initials written in the upper right-hand corner of each filled out page. Occasionally she would write a one- or two-word comment: "Excellent" or "Good work."

I remember the first TFA recruiting poster I saw. It was a black-and-white photograph of an African American man in a loose tie standing in front of a chalkboard facing excited students of color. There was no explanation, just a phone number. I wanted in. I wanted to be standing in front of a chalkboard, dazzling the students before me with new information. I wanted to love these kids, and I wanted them to love me. I wanted to teach them, give them something they would not have had without me. I had a savior complex, and I (like TFA, I think) assumed good teaching was simply the conveying of content by caring, competent people. TFA depended on my believing this was true, otherwise there's no way I would have signed up to teach in Compton for two years.

My desire to do well despite not knowing how to teach got in my way. I wanted to "get a good grade" more than I wanted constructive criticism—more, even, than I wanted help. I was observed several times a year by the principal. Her visits were announced beforehand, so, as I did for my mentor's visits, I prepared myself and my students. I always chose a lesson I already knew worked. I talked to my students and told them the principal was going to visit and that this was our opportunity to show her how smart and well behaved we were. I was never a better teacher and my students were never better behaved than on the days when my principal visited.

I still wonder what might have happened if I had let her see what real days in my classroom were like. Days I was so frustrated with the never-ending noise in my classroom that I stopped in the middle of a lesson, kneeled on the rug, and held my head in my hands. Days I had to scrap a lesson because I didn't have the necessary supplies because I'd woken up late and hadn't had time to stop at the store on my way to school. Days I yelled. Days I made all my students put their heads on their desks so I could have five minutes of quiet. Days I sent the most difficult students to another classroom for the whole day because I couldn't handle one more minute of disruptive behavior. Days I wasted my students' time with stupid coloring activities because I ran out of lessons. Days I cried. Days I threw away piles of turned-in homework because I was too exhausted to grade it. The stories collected in this chapter offer images of such real days in my classroom.

One of the things that troubled me the most when I was in Compton was that I was practicing how to teach on real children. I learned by doing. I learned how to teach in a real classroom, filled with brilliant, difficult, troubled students, all by myself. I was thirty-six children's real first grade teacher, and then I was thirty-six more children's real second grade teacher. I was the adult in charge of their classrooms, but often I felt like I was in a play, as if I had stepped onto the stage in the role of "teacher." Usually I felt like I had forgotten my lines.

Monday. 7:45 a.m. Madison Elementary School. Tony Raymond walked next to the line of my first grade students waiting to go into the classroom and jabbed each student he passed with the point of his pencil. When we got inside the room, Tony called Johnny a "fat punk" and told Carmen to "shut up," words never allowed in Room 8. Then he refused to sit on the carpet with the rest of the class and instead sat at his desk and kicked it with his shoe. I looked at the clock on the wall. It was only 8:00.

At age six, Tony had already been abandoned—with his four brothers and sisters—by his drug-addicted mother, who called (as she did that very Monday morning) each time she got clean. Tony had curly brown hair and was missing his top right front tooth. He had a smile that came easily and unexpectedly and lit up his entire face, especially when we read Tomie dePaola's book *Big Anthony and the Magic Ring*. He loved to read Big Anthony's part to the entire class. When Tony turned seven, I gave him dePaola's *The Art Lesson* because Tony, like the main character in the story, loved to draw. And I loved to watch him draw. He would bend his head close to the page, grip his pencil, and slowly and carefully create magnificent pictures: kites, smiling children, dinosaurs, birds, brilliant suns. Every day he brought me a new drawing he had copied from *The Art Lesson* and asked me to put it on my refrigerator at home. Then he would ask me if I still had the drawing of the boy with the kite he gave me at the beginning of the year. When I would tell him it was still hanging on my refrigerator, he would smile. And I would feel like crying.

Tony and his brothers and sisters lived with their grandmother, Maya Lively. "This isn't what I imagined for myself," she told me during our parent-teacher conference in the fall. "I did this already. I raised my kids once. I didn't expect to have to raise my kids' kids, too." She had been a manager at a department store in New York City when her son called her and asked her to move to California. He and his wife had separated, and the five young children had gone to live with his wife, Tony's mother. Then the mother started using drugs and began to abuse her children. Tony's father wanted Mrs. Lively to move to Compton to take care of his kids. And she did. She had to. There was no one else.

Tony's grandmother and I talked almost every day. After school, Tony and I would hold hands as we walked to meet her and the rest of her grandchildren piled in their station wagon. Leaning into the car window, I would tell her how Tony had behaved in school that day—if he had finished his work, hit any other students, followed directions. Sometimes when Tony had a good day in school, he would pretend to look upset and I would pretend to look mad so we could surprise his grandmother when we told her how well behaved he had been. Mrs. Lively and I spent months analyzing his behavior, trying to figure out what he was thinking, how he was feeling, how to help him handle his outbursts, his intense emotions.

One day he behaved perfectly. The next morning Mrs. Lively came to see me before school.

"He had a good day yesterday, didn't he?" she said.

"Yes," I said. "A perfect day. What happened?"

"I talked to him about it, and he said he just really liked wearing his tennis shoes."

I laughed and said, "You keep him in those shoes then, OK?"

"Oh, you know I will," she said. "You know I will."

Tony loved to play basketball. He gave me a wallet-sized photograph of himself wearing his team jersey and holding a basketball under one arm. In the basketball picture, he looks the exact opposite of the way he looks in our class picture. In the class picture, he is glaring at the camera with his lips pursed so tightly that they are almost invisible. His fists are clenched and at his sides. He looks ready to explode. In the basketball picture, Tony is smiling, standing in front of a backdrop of Lakers Stadium with a basketball under his arm and his other hand on his hip. When he handed me the photograph, I turned it over and found this inscription in his grandmother's handwriting: "To Ms. Sentilles, Thank you for caring. With love always, Tony J. Raymond." I still carry his picture in my wallet.

Tony's best friend was Prince Stephens. Most visitors to my first grade classroom initially thought Prince was a girl. He wore his hair slicked back in a braided ponytail. His brother did, too. From behind, they looked exactly the same.

Prince's brother was infamous at Madison Elementary School. And most teachers expected Prince to be as difficult as his brother. When I received my roster and other teachers realized Prince was in my class, they would shake their heads and say something like, "Oh, no, you got the other Stephens boy. Good luck."

But while Prince's brother roamed around school, ran away, and hit his teacher, Prince, inside my classroom, was pretty well behaved. Outside the classroom was a different story. At recess, on the yard waiting to eat lunch, inside the cafeteria, he swore, kicked, hit, stole. Once I was called to the yard because Prince had found a dead rat in a puddle underneath the monkey bars and was swinging it around by its tail, brandishing it at students standing near him.

Prince's mother picked him up every day after school, and if he had been especially difficult or violent at recess, I would tell her what had happened. She would listen and nod, occasionally uttering a high-pitched "uh-huh," and when I finished, she would say, "Peee-rince, how many times do I have to hear things like that?" Then she would hand him a dollar to buy something at the PTA candy table.

Rumor had it that one day she got in a fight with the principal, Mrs. Redding. Mrs. Redding always spoke to parents in a quiet voice, almost a whisper. Her theory was that if she stayed calm and quiet, the parents would be forced to meet her tone. She spoke to teachers that way, too. She tried to use elementary school classroom discipline on adults. I didn't even talk to my *first graders* that way. Her tone was annoying and patronizing. I guess Prince's mother didn't like it either, and she let the principal know that in no uncertain terms. I heard that the principal had to call the police.

Both Tony and Prince were extraordinary artists, but I knew they shared more than a love for drawing. They were little boys who sometimes seemed more like silent old men. They didn't talk to each other much, at least not in front of me, but they were almost always together, standing next to each other or drawing side by side. Their drawings were radically different. Tony loved to draw Tomie dePaola's character Anthony, smiling. Prince loved drawing Power Rangers. Power Rangers fighting, kicking, shooting, and punching. His artwork was filled with images of guns and knives and blood.

I saw Prince smile only a handful of times during the year. One of those times was when I brought in modeling clay at the end of a unit on dinosaurs. Each student got to create a dinosaur out of clay. Prince made a tyrannosaurus rex, a triceratops, and a pterodactyl in the time it took other students just to decide which dinosaur they were going to try to make. Each of his sculptured dinosaurs was more perfect than the last. They looked exactly like the dinosaurs in drawings at natural history museums.

A few days after the dinosaur project, Prince and his brother went into our classroom while I was outside on recess duty. One of my students saw them and ran to get me from the yard. When I got to the classroom, only Prince was there. His brother, it seemed, had snuck into the classroom, where he overturned chairs, took books off the shelves and threw them on the floor, and threatened to smash the clay dinosaurs still drying on the ledge above the bookshelves. Prince had followed his brother into the room—I think to protect the dinosaurs. When I walked into the room, Prince was sitting on the floor holding one of the dinosaurs he had made in his lap. It was broken, and he was trying to put it back together. When he saw me, he started to cry. I opened my arms and hugged him. It was the only time he let me hug him all year.

Mrs. Redding, the principal at Madison, probably needed a hug as badly as Prince did. She was hated by almost every teacher under her supervision. Mrs. Redding was quite short, barely five feet. She could not have weighed more than ninety pounds. She dressed impeccably and always wore her hair in a tight high ponytail on the top of her head. She had a habit of pulling the ponytail in half in order to draw the rubber band closer to her head. Once it was tight enough, she would arrange her curls in a circle on top of her head. She refused to learn the names of the adults in students' families. She simply called them by their familial role—grandmother, mother, father, guardian. I cringed every time I heard her speak to someone. "Grandmother, you really need to be on time to pick up your children," or "Mother, do you think you could be a bit more quiet in the entryway?" She also whispered to people when they got angry. The louder one spoke, the quieter she became. Parents grew to hate her so much that she eventually needed a police escort from her office to her parked car every day after school.

She was new to Madison the same year I was. She came at the end of September to replace a principal who was promoted. On her first day, she gathered all the teachers in the cafeteria for a staff meeting. Without saying a word, she started handing out graphs and markers. She then organized us by grade level and asked us to please color in the graphs together. They were bar graphs representing Madison students' performance on the California Achievement Test (CAT-5). We colored. She collected the graphs. And then she hung them around the room using pushpins.

"Not very good," she said when all the graphs were hung

around us. She clucked her tongue and shook her head. "Not very good. You're going to have to do better than that."

Halfway through the school year, sometime in January, several veteran teachers at Madison held a secret meeting and wrote a "no confidence letter," asking the district to fire her. I was approached by another teacher who asked me to sign the letter. I refused. I had not written the letter, and I was not sure I had no confidence in Mrs. Redding. Immediately I became almost as unpopular as Mrs. Redding.

The teachers held another secret meeting, and everyone, including me, was invited. I sat across the table from Mrs. Glass, whose classroom was next door to mine. She was one of the only teachers at the school who ever offered me teaching advice. Several times she pulled me from the hallway into her classroom. "Ms. Sentilles," she would say. "You really ought to wear a slip." Mrs. Glass looked at the assembled faculty, and then she began to speak, looking directly at me. "Some of you are being babies. You're too young to know what's good for you. It's time to grow up, babies, and sign this letter."

I still refused.

Three weeks later, several people in suits showed up at Madison and called teachers, four at a time, into a room at the end of a row of portable buildings to meet with them. The secretary, Mrs. Gutierrez, knocked on my classroom door in the middle of our math lesson, told me to take my students to recess, and then to go to Room 32. I did as I was told. I walked into the room and an older man told me to sit down.

"So," he said, looking at the four of us sitting there. "What did you sign?"

We looked at him.

"What did you sign?" he asked again, obviously annoyed already.

"What do you mean?" I asked.

"What did you sign? Your signatures are not attached to the original document. I can only assume you had no idea what you were signing. The ringleaders here must have attached your names to a document different from the one you thought you were signing."

"Well," I said, calmly, "why don't you tell us what the letter says, and we will tell you if it is different than the one we signed."

"Why don't you, little missy, just tell me what you signed?"

"No."

"I don't think any of you knew what you were doing," he said to me, rolling his eyes.

"You think we are dumb enough to sign something we didn't see before we signed it? I find that insulting. We are all grownups here. Why don't you just show us the letter, and we can get this resolved."

"How dare you tell me what to do! Who do you think you are? What kind of person comes into this district and signs a no confidence letter against her boss and then refuses to cooperate?" He shouted at me, waving his finger back and forth in front of my face. All of his words started running together. He hated me because he assumed I had signed the letter; the faculty hated me because I hadn't.

I don't remember how I got out of that room. Somehow,

though, I found myself outside. I leaned against one of the portable buildings and sobbed. I felt completely alone. I pressed my forehead against the crumbling wood. I remember noticing the peeling white paint and finding it, somehow, beautiful.

I looked at my watch. Almost an hour had passed since my students had been sent to recess. I started walking quickly toward the yard. I passed Ms. Tyler's fifth grade classroom. The door was open. One of her students, Shawn, saw me and could tell I had been crying. He stood up from his desk and ran out of his classroom toward me. He flung his arms around my waist. "Are you okay, Ms. Sentilles? Is someone bothering you?" His hug was exactly what I needed.

Shawn's gesture drew the attention of my students. Boredom had scattered them around the campus to search for something, anything, to do. From all directions, they started running toward me. A few feet in front of me they stopped. They could tell I was upset.

"Oh, no!" shouted Carlos. "You lost your job!" Then I had thirty-six students around me, hugging me, telling me they loved me, and begging me not to leave.

"No," I said. "I did not lose my job, and I'm not going anywhere."

Later that afternoon, I went to the front office to sign out. Mrs. Redding was sitting in her office, and she heard me come in. She came out to see me.

"Ms. Sentilles," she said. "Thank you."

"For what?" I asked.

"Thank you for not signing that silly letter."

"Oh, that."

"You know," she said, tightening her ponytail and arranging the curls on the top of her head, "not signing that letter will definitely bring you another jewel in your crown in heaven."

✎ ✎ ✎

Murielle Smith, one of the jewels in my first grade class, saw the world differently than most people, and she used creative words to describe what she saw. I loved her words, and I kept track of all the strange and wonderful things she said, scribbling them on scraps of paper around the room so I could remember them exactly. She was cross-eyed. She had a slight limp that sometimes looked like a limp and sometimes looked like a spring in her step. She didn't quite bend her knees all the way when she walked, and when she ran, she galloped, always putting her right leg in front of her left. Murielle tried to balance on crayons. She scratched her skin where she thought mosquitoes might bite her. And whenever she tripped, which was often, she would say, "Whoa, my shoe's coming loose again."

After recess on the first day of school, I asked my first graders to draw a picture of themselves playing on the yard. When they finished drawing, they were supposed to raise their hands, I would then go to their table, and they would dictate to me what was happening in the picture while I wrote their words down for them. Most students drew themselves playing on the slide or playing tag with a friend. They would say something simple like, "I am sliding and waving to my teacher." When I came to

Murielle's desk and looked at her picture, I couldn't tell what she had drawn. So I said, "Murielle, why don't you tell me about your picture? It looks beautiful."

In her distinct low, gravelly voice, she said, "House, burning on fire. Pink jellyfish swimming in my eyes. Christopher's in there, and he's green and white."

My sudden intake of breath must have been audible. "Wow, Murielle. That's great. I'm just going to write your mom a little note on the back of your picture, OK?"

Later that week, I asked my first grade students to create self-portraits. When they finished drawing themselves, they were supposed to write their names and ages below the picture. After they had been working on the portraits for about fifteen minutes I said, "OK, it's time to stop drawing yourselves and start writing your names."

Murielle said, "You want me to stop drawing hamburgers now?"

"No," I said, "I want you to stop drawing your self-portrait."

"So," Murielle said, "like I said, you want me to stop drawing hamburgers now? Do you like my hamburgers?"

I walked over to see what she was drawing. She had drawn a face in the middle of her paper with six pieces of curly hair flowing out of the top of the head, like some sort of Medusa. Surrounding the head were several hamburgers, floating in an arch. "Yes, Murielle. It's time to stop drawing hamburgers now."

During one art lesson when the class was painting, Murielle got green paint all over her hand. She had a small cut on her hand, and the green paint made the cut look green too.

She walked up to me and said, "I got a cut at my dad's house. Wanna see?"

"Sure, Murielle," I said. She showed me the sliver of a cut, and I kissed two of my fingers and put them near her cut. Whenever my students were hurt, I kissed my fingers and put them near the place where they were hurt. Some students thought this was magic and made the pain go away immediately. Others just thought I was weird.

Murielle thought I was weird. She said, "Kissing my green sore, huh?"

I started to laugh. "You're really funny, Murielle," I said.

She looked right at me and said, "But you're not funny, are you?"

That made me laugh harder, and she asked, "Are you laughing at me? Are you laughing at me?"

"No, I'm not laughing at you," I said. "I'm just laughing."

"I've got to get out of here!" she shouted, and then she ran out of the room with her hands still covered in green paint.

At the end of the first quarter, I filled out report cards for my first graders. I had to give them letter grades for several subjects: reading, handwriting, math, social studies, science, physical education, art. It seemed ridiculous to give letter grades to first graders. I remembered Excellent, Satisfactory, or Unsatisfactory on my first grade report card. I gave most of my students As and Bs. My goal was to encourage them, to help them feel smart. I thought if they believed they were smart, and if they believed I believed they were smart, they would feel good about school and do well. I agonized over the comment section on the report cards. I tried to make sure my comments showed my students' parents how much I valued, knew, and loved their children. I spent hours and hours on my first set of report cards.

On Murielle's report card I wrote, "I imagine Murielle will be a famous poet someday. She has a gift for language and is extremely creative. For now, though, she needs to concentrate on her handwriting and staying in her seat." I was proud of my comments about her. They were my favorite.

Before I gave my students their report cards to take home, I had to turn them in to Mrs. Redding so she could look at them. The day after I gave her the report cards, I found a note in my box: Come see me, Ms. Sentilles. Mrs. Redding often left notes in teachers' boxes, and they rarely meant good news.

I knocked on her door and went into her office. "Good morning, Ms. Sentilles," she said. In Compton, it was considered extremely rude to jump right into conversation. You always had to say "Good morning" or "Hello" or "Good afternoon" first, even when what you were about to say was rude.

"Good morning, Mrs. Redding."

"Your grades are way too high. My husband and I figured out that the percentage of As you gave was over 70 percent. You must do your report cards all over again."

"I did them that way because I think it's silly to give anyone a low grade after the first ten weeks in school. I want my students to feel good about themselves and about school," I said.

"That's not the point of a report card, Ms. Sentilles."

"That's the point of *my* report cards, Mrs. Redding."

"Well, speaking from twenty years' experience as a classroom teacher—and I know it's only your first time filling out report cards—I have to let you know that it is important for students to know that they have to work for grades, and it's important to give them room to improve. These grades are too high. Do them again, and give them back to me tomorrow."

I was furious, but I didn't know how to argue with her twenty years of experience. I had ten weeks of experience. I was as new to first grade as my students. I wanted someone to give me good grades, and I certainly wasn't getting them. I left the office and went back to my classroom. I started looking through the pile of report cards Mrs. Redding had returned to me. She had put little yellow Post-Its all over them. On Murielle's report card, she had stuck a note on the comment section where I had written that I thought Murielle would be a poet. The note said, "This is your opinion. Only facts belong on report cards."

My mother came to visit my classroom at the end of my first year as a teacher. She brought each student a new book, individually wrapped and inscribed with a personal note from her. She was most excited about meeting Murielle. Murielle was working on a drawing when my mom sat down next to her at her desk. "Murielle," my mom said, "I have been noticing that you draw a lot of rectangles in your art. Can you tell me about them?"

Murielle looked at my mom. "Don't you see the holes? That's Swiss cheese! I love to draw Swiss cheese!" My mom laughed, hugged Murielle, and said, "Of course, Murielle. Swiss cheese. It looks amazing."

At the end of the school year, Murielle's family moved to Long Beach. She left school one week before the rest of the students. On her last day, I hugged her and started to cry. "I am going to miss you, Murielle."

"Miss me?" she asked. "I only came because my mama made me. Otherwise I would have run out." And with that, she ran out my classroom door.

✎ ✎ ✎

I often took students on trips outside the classroom. I took them to museums, movies, parks, and libraries. I took Enrique Palacios to the annual Teach for America student appreciation day. I drove to his house to pick him up, and Enrique and his mother were waiting outside for me. They were standing next to an enormous rosebush, filled with blooming roses. Enrique's smile was so big I could see all his teeth.

"Hi, Ms. Sentilles," he said.

"Hi, Enrique. You look so handsome."

"I got a new outfit for spending the day with you," he said. He was wearing a red, white, and blue shorts outfit and brand-new white tennis shoes. His shirt was tucked tightly into his shorts.

Enrique looked almost like a jolly old man in a child's body. I imagined he combed his hair the same way my grandfather did: standing in front of the mirror, a towel wrapped around his waist, wetting his small comb in the faucet and running it through his hair until it was perfect. He was an only child and lived with his mother, who worked two jobs. He was the most well-behaved student in my classroom. He loved school. He always did his work and never fought with the other students. Enrique had one gold tooth, which was almost always visible because he was always smiling. For Halloween, he was Groucho

Marx. I laughed out loud seeing Enrique with wild curly hair and a big (fake) cigar sticking out of his mouth.

Time management was extremely important to Enrique. Several times a day he would check in with me about what we were going to do next and just how much time I imagined that activity would take. "Ms. Sentilles, do you think we will get to art today?" or "Ms. Sentilles, how much time will we be doing math?" or "Ms. Sentilles, do you realize we have been doing this activity for twenty-five minutes?" One afternoon, I was teaching a lesson on how to tell time. I had my students create clocks out of paper plates. We wrote the numbers around the edge of the plate, made an hour hand and a minute hand out of construction paper, and then used a gold-colored brad to connect them to the plates. Voilà. A clock.

After we finished creating the clocks, we had a race to find the time. I would announce a time, and each group of students would have to work together to set their clocks to the correct time. I kept score. At the end of the activity, I told the students to put their clocks in their desks so we could use them later. Enrique raised his hand.

"Yes, Enrique?"

"Can we keep the clocks?"

"Of course," I said. "At the end of our unit on time you can take them home with you."

Enrique could not contain his excitement. He leaped out of his chair and screamed, "I love you too much!"

I spelled Denver Carraway's name wrong for the first two weeks of second grade at Garvey Elementary School. I wrote "Carrway" on her journal. I wrote "Carrway" on her homework folder. I wrote "Carrway" on the notes I sent home. And every day she would come up to my desk at the end of the day and hand me a scrap of paper with her name written the right way on it: Denver T. Carraway. It took me two weeks to believe her. But I finally got it right.

Denver made sure she hated everyone before they could hate her. She hit before she would be hit. She yelled before she would be yelled at. This way she made sure she knew how the world worked. She controlled what seemed beyond her control. But no matter how much she hurt other people, she could never hurt them as much as she already hurt.

Denver was born addicted to drugs. The only time her mother came to school was to ask the principal for money. Denver tested me. She refused to go to recess, and then she refused to return to the classroom after recess. She hit students. She called them names. She refused to start projects, and then, once she had decided to start, she refused to stop when the lesson was over. Denver reminded me daily that I was not in control. When I sent her to the office after she pulled a boy's pants down and punched a student officer, and the principal sent her back with a note that said "Please keep her until the end of the day," Denver reminded me that the principal was not in control either.

Denver loomed large in my imagination; she seemed older and taller than she was in reality. She wore her dark hair in three sets of braids, pulled high and off her face. She arrived at school each day wearing the optional school uniform: navy blue skirt and white, short-sleeved blouse. By the end of the day, her clean white blouse would be untucked, missing buttons, and stained with something from the cafeteria.

Denver, her two brothers, George and Rickie, and her sister, Leah, lived with their grandmother, a large woman who had trouble walking and always seemed to be out of breath. I don't know how she managed to take care of four children. She could barely walk across the campus and up the two steps to my classroom, but her grandchildren came to school clean, well dressed, and well fed. Watching Denver's grandmother make her way across the black asphalt, her grandchildren running circles around her, yelling at or hitting each other, I tried to imagine what went on inside their house. This woman, like so many women in Compton, had already raised her own children, and now she was raising her children's children. I think she was exhausted. It was hard for her to breathe.

I think the role I was least prepared to play as a teacher was disciplinarian. I was forced to be a drill sergeant, caring about things I never thought I would care about—straight lines, inside voices, broken crayons. Being in charge of thirty-six children in one classroom made everything seem important to me. Each little rebellion—and to me, they were just that, rebellions—seemed huge. How dare a child take her neighbor's pencil, get out of her seat, not put her hands at her sides when she walked in line?

Denver took away any semblance of control I thought I had. And this infuriated me. I felt helpless, desperate, irrational. She drove me crazy, literally crazy. Denver didn't respond to threats or choices or punishments. When I yelled at her, her eyes would get a faraway look and a slight smile would spread across her face. She hit. She ignored. She bullied. And there was nothing I could do to stop her.

Every day on my way to school, I pictured Denver in my mind. I thought about her grandmother, about her missing mother, about what it must be like to spend time in her house, and I would promise myself that there was nothing she could do to upset me. She is only seven, I would tell myself. She is acting out of her own pain. It is not a personal attack. I am older than she is. There is nothing Denver can do today to make me mad. I will remain calm.

I even prayed for Denver in church. I prayed for the strength to respond to Denver differently. Kneeling in the pew, reviewing the week's events in my mind, what was more disturbing to me than Denver's behavior was my own. I had screamed at a broken seven-year-old. I had glared at her. Humiliated her in front of her classmates. Mocked her. Every day, I met her violence with my violence, her woundedness with my wounding, her anger with my anger. I fulfilled her image of how the world worked. People hated. People yelled.

Then, one day in late November, Denver and I changed. Denver was in trouble. I'm not sure what she had done or how I responded, but I do remember that I made her stay with me in the classroom while the rest of the class went to lunch and then recess. For students at Garvey Elementary School going late to lunch was traumatic. Teachers did their best to control what went on inside their classrooms, but they were not able to control what happened outside their classrooms. Terror reigned at recess. There was nothing for the students to do. The "yard" consisted of broken glass, rusted metal bars, tetherball poles with no balls attached to the strings, and a chain link fence. There was usually only one teacher—possibly two—in charge of over three hundred bored, angry, scared children. There were no consequences for bad behavior. Nothing happened if a student hit another student. Nothing happened if a student used bad language.

Because I made Denver go ten minutes late to lunch, she knew she was about to enter the chaos of the playground unaccompanied by the rest of her classmates. Her position as the toughest person in the classroom made her safe on the yard during second grade recess. Most second graders knew not to bother her. But the day I made her go late to lunch, she would be on her own, without her friends, without people who recognized her role as the classroom bully. And I think that scared her. It would have scared me.

That day, I kept her in the room for ten minutes. When I decided it was time for her to go to lunch—and time for me to grab my lunch in the fifteen minutes I had left before I had to pick up my students after recess—she refused to go. I was tired and hungry. "Denver, let's go. It's time for you to go eat," I said.

She did not move from her desk.

"Denver, I don't care if you eat or not, but you have to get up, get out of this room, and go to the cafeteria."

No movement from Denver.

"Denver, I am leaving now and so are you. Get up now."

She got out of her seat and walked toward the door I held

open for her. She slid under my arm and out the door. Instead of walking toward the cafeteria, which was directly in front of our portable classroom building, she turned and flattened herself against the front of our building.

I had run out of patience. It was no longer teacher and student. Ms. Sentilles, the teacher, was gone. It was Sarah and Denver. "Whatever, Denver," I said. I left her standing there and went back into the classroom to get my turkey sandwich, Lays potato chips, and Dr. Pepper, the lunch I ate every single day while I was teaching in Compton. At that moment I was sick of her. Sick of dealing with her. Sick of her ruining my days and my students' days.

Suddenly I heard a loud noise. Denver was kicking the side of our classroom and shouting, "I hate my teacher!" *KICK* "I hate my teacher!" *KICK* "I hate my teacher!" *KICK* "I hate my teacher!"

I went back outside and started yelling, too.

"I hate my teacher!"—"Who do you think you are?"—"I hate my teacher!"—"You can't kick our classroom!"—"I hate my teacher!"—"Cut it out!"—"I hate my teacher!"—"Get yourself back in that room!"

For some reason, she came back inside with me. We were both angry. I looked at her. She looked at me. And in that moment of pain and fury, something clicked inside of me.

I think she expected me to continue yelling. I think I expected myself to continue yelling. But I didn't. Instead I started talking to her. "Denver," I said, "I just want you to know that I think about you all the time. Every day on my way to school, I think to myself, 'There is nothing Denver can do to upset me today.' Even though I sometimes do not like the things you do, that doesn't mean that I don't like you. I love you, Denver. I want you to know that. No matter what, I love you."

She looked at me. I opened my arms to hug her. She wrapped her arms around my waist and started to cry.

I never had another problem with Denver inside Room 18.

Every day after school, Denver walked home with her sister and two brothers. Her house was just a few blocks away from Garvey. Toward the end of the year, she started staying after school. After I had cleaned my room and was walking to my car to drive home, she would suddenly run across the campus toward me. It would be almost 5:00 in the afternoon. School got out at 2:15. "What are you still doing here, Denver?" I would ask, as if I didn't already know that she had walked back to school at the time when she thought I would be about to leave.

"Leah, Rickie, and George left me today, Ms. Sentilles," she would say, smiling.

"Really, Denver? So what would you like me to do for you?"

"Could you drive me home, Ms. Sentilles?"

"Of course, Denver," I would say. And she would climb into the front seat, fasten her seatbelt, and smile. Denver loved riding in the car with me, and I loved to drive her home. Her appearance at the end of each day felt like an embrace.

I felt no such embrace at 7:45 a.m. on the first day of my second year of teaching. I was a new teacher at Garvey Elementary

School, and I was nervous. I stood on the number 18 painted on the black asphalt in front of my portable classroom and held a sign that read "Welcome to Room 18" with my name written across the bottom. I looked around, trying to pick out the students who would become mine.

Then I saw Obsidian Banks and her mother. Her mother looked at me, looked up at the sign I was holding, looked down at the registration paper she had for Obsidian, looked back at me, and said, "Oh, no."

I took this as a bad sign, but I introduced myself anyway. "Hi, I'm Sarah Sentilles. I think I'm your daughter's teacher."

"Oh, no," she said again, waving her finger back and forth in front of me. "Oh, no. I'm sorry, but this will not do at all. I will have to have my daughter switched into another class. No offense, but this will not do at all. Oh, no."

Helplessly I blurted, "But you don't even know me. Please give me a chance."

Mrs. Banks drew in a deep breath, looked at her daughter, looked back at me, and then said reluctantly, "OK. I'll think about it."

Obsidian didn't walk, she skipped. She was the shortest second grader in my class, and every inch of her was packed with energy and attitude. She had an amazing laugh. I have a photograph of her above my desk: with her head thrown back, she's clapping her hands and laughing with her mouth wide open. She was a ringleader and exercised her power over the entire class, making people laugh as easily as she made them cry.

Despite our rocky first moments, Obsidian's mother and I developed a good relationship quickly. When Obsidian got in trouble at school—when she pulled down a boy's pants at recess, when she teased the girl who had lice—I sometimes called her mother. Minutes later, she would arrive at the classroom door and look directly at Obsidian, who was cowering in her seat. Then she would turn to me and say in a voice loud enough for the entire class to hear, "Ms. Sentilles, she knows her mama don't play that game. No. I don't play that game at all."

The first time Mrs. Banks visited my classroom, she walked to my desk and opened her purse to show me the black leather belt coiled inside. "She knows what she's got coming," she said to me. "There's no need to act up in school when she's supposed to be learning. We don't have that kind of time." After that first visit, whenever Mrs. Banks came to the classroom she would hold her purse tightly against her hip and pat it as she looked at Obsidian. She seemed to be reminding me and Obsidian what was inside. "You know what's coming for you at home," she would say, and I would look away, ashamed to be helpless, judgmental, and somehow responsible for what was about to happen to Obsidian.

The day after her mother's classroom visits, Obsidian would find me in the morning before class to apologize. "I'm sorry, really sorry, Ms. Sentilles," she would say. And then she would pull me down close to her so she could whisper in my ear, "You know my mama didn't whip me last night. She really didn't. She just talked to me."

I chose to believe her.

Every year across California, public school students take the California Achievement Test, known as the CAT-5. The first year I taught in Compton my students were horribly unprepared for the test. My second year, I was determined not to let this happen again. I started preparing my students for the CAT-5 four months before the test date. No one would give me any test preparation materials, so I invented my own way of preparing my kids. I used the test booklet that I had stolen the year before, and I used my own creativity. Every day we completed five language arts questions in the morning and five mathematics questions before lunch. Before the students answered the questions, we would run through a verbal routine:

Me: What are we practicing for?

Students: The CAT-5!

Me: What are we going to get 100 on?

Students: The CAT-5!

Me: What test is going to show the world how smart we are?

Students: The CAT-5!

Then we would begin to solve the questions. We practiced and practiced. They took practice tests at home. They did practice tests during language arts centers. Soon my students could answer any kind of question I threw at them—synonyms, antonyms, sums, patterns, reading comprehension, vocabulary, spelling, multiplication.

No one practiced harder for the CAT-5 than Obsidian. She could not get enough. She wanted to do extra questions. She practiced at home with her mother. She reminded me all the time that she was the fastest student on the math section of the test.

When the time came for the real test, we knew we were ready.

We could not have been more wrong.

During the week of testing, I felt as though my efforts to prepare my students and my students' hard work were being mocked. The Friday before the testing began, I was given the teacher's manual and a schedule. I took the manual home and read it over the weekend. Garvey Elementary School seemed to have chosen to ignore all of the advice outlined in the manual: "Never give a test following a weekend or a holiday." We started on Monday. "Give one or two sections of the test each day over a two-week period." We gave four to five sections a day for one week. We had to rush through the test, I was told, because "they" (I assumed the "they" referred to the state administrators) had given us only two weeks to test all the students. The teachers had one week to test the students; the instructional assistants were given the second week to "clean up" the books and code them.

Monday morning, I went into the office to pick up the test booklets for my students taking the test in English. As I walked across the campus from the office to my classroom, Obsidian ran up to me. She could barely contain her excitement. "The CAT-5 is today! The CAT-5 is today!" she shouted as she grabbed my empty hand. "I'm so excited. My mom said if I do well we will go somewhere fun. She is going to be so proud of me. I've been practicing and practicing."

After sending the students who were taking the test in Spanish to the cafeteria, I gave each remaining student a handful of M&Ms. We called the M&Ms brain food. They could eat the M&Ms when they felt tired or stuck on a particular question during the test. Then I began to administer the test. I tried to follow the testing schedule, but after I had been testing for over four hours, I had to stop even though I hadn't completed the required sections. By the third section of the test—during the third hour of testing—my students were falling apart. Elise started to eat her test booklet. Sandra refused to answer any more questions. Bobby just started guessing the answers because he was tired of reading the questions.

Watching Obsidian struggle through the test was the most difficult part for me. She was trying so hard. She stopped occasionally and looked at me, wide-eyed. I walked to her table and whispered to her, "Just do your best, Obsidian. Just do your best." A few times she started to cry. She said, "I can't do this, Ms. Sentilles. I can't do this test at all."

After the fourth hour, I stopped giving the test and let my students go out for recess. While the other students ran out the door, Obsidian stayed behind. She was crying. "My mom is going to be so upset," she said. "I tried my best, but it was so long. I didn't know how to do a lot of it. I'm not going to get 100. I feel dumb." I tried to explain how smart she was, that the test was just one test and really did not show how well she had been doing all year in school. I assured her that I knew she was smart and her mom knew she was smart. But my words could not undo the feelings of shame, failure, and frustration that the test had produced in her.

I was furious. When I dismissed my students at the end of the day. I saw the assistant principal, Mrs. Wallace, and I started to yell at her. "Who created that ridiculous test schedule?" I demanded. "Who thought it was a good idea to ignore the manual's advice to give only one or two sections each day?"

Mrs. Wallace just looked at me.

I was screaming now. "Who actually thought it was normal to expect seven-year-olds to sit through over four hours of testing?"

She continued to stand there, holding her clipboard and looking at me.

"I am so angry I can't stand it. My kids knew so much. We practiced and prepared for so long. And we might as well have done nothing because their scores will say they knew nothing. Why did we even bother?"

"Well," she said, "everyone's entitled to her own opinion." Then she turned and walked away.

The test schedule was probably not Mrs. Wallace's fault. I don't know who created it, and it probably doesn't matter. What matters is that there was nothing standard about those tests at all. And I wanted to write that all over my students' tests. I wanted to write big bold disclaimers. *We didn't have enough time to take the tests. We crammed all the testing into one week. Sometimes we don't have enough pencils. We had thirty-six students stuffed into one room with no instructional assistant and no windows.*

I was never shown the results of the tests. Maybe my students performed brilliantly. What's more likely, however, is that the results confirmed what many think they already know. *See, children in Compton can't learn. They really are slow. They're way behind everyone else in math and reading.* Probably no one looking at the test scores asked why they were so low or visited my overcrowded classroom and saw the absence of books. No one met Obsidian and saw what a good reader she was and that she already knew multiplication. It was easier to look at how the students failed than to look at how we failed our students.

Obsidian and her best friend, Denver, usually met me at my car when I pulled into the school's driveway every morning. One day they weren't there, and as I got out of the car, I saw them hiding in a corner next to the nurse's office. I walked over to see them.

"What's wrong?" I asked.

Denver looked at me and then pointed to Obsidian and started laughing. "Look at what she's wearing," Denver said between outbursts.

Obsidian looked adorable to me, but I knew adorable was not the look she was going for. She was wearing navy blue shorts and suspenders and brand-new white tennis shoes. I think it was the suspenders that were so upsetting.

"I think you look beautiful, Obsidian," I said as I put my arm around her. "And you know I'm the queen of fashion."

My comment made Denver laugh even harder. She clearly didn't think I was the queen of fashion. Denver stopped laughing suddenly and looked me straight in the eye. In a very serious voice she said, "Ms. Sentilles, you forgot about your toes." Obsidian and Denver made fun of my toes every time I wore sandals to school. They thought my toes were just way too long. According to Denver, my long toes put me in no position to be giving anyone fashion advice.

I laughed and said, "Oh, yeah, my toes. But I still think

Obsidian looks beautiful. I have always wanted a pair of suspenders."

"Well, you can have mine," Obsidian said, tugging on her suspenders as she and Denver ran ahead of me to our classroom.

On the last day of school, Mrs. Banks and I hugged each other. She said, "Remember that first day? You said, 'Please give me a chance.' I'm sure glad I did." Hers was one of the best compliments I ever received as a teacher.

Kevin James, one of my second grade students, was given chance after chance after chance in my classroom. He withdrew from school, came back to school, and withdrew again every few weeks. Secretly, I was happy whenever I found the blue withdrawal slip with his name written on it in my teacher's box. Kevin was a very difficult student. He hit other students, rarely did his work, could not read, and was extremely stubborn. Whenever I talked to him his eyes seemed to glaze over, and he would smile with his mouth slightly open and his head tilted to one side. I could never tell if he heard a word I said. Kevin's behavior made more sense to me when I met his mother. When I talked with her, I realized hers was the same expression I saw on Kevin's face: eyes glazed, lips slightly parted, head tilted. She rarely responded verbally to anything I said. She would just nod her head, take Kevin's hand in hers, and walk away.

Although Kevin almost never did the assignment that the rest of the class was doing, he worked extremely carefully on whatever he did choose to do. He covered most of his papers—

math worksheets, language arts handouts, or spelling tests—
with heart-shaped balloons. He might not have been able to
name all the letters in the alphabet, but he could write each one
beautifully. On the rare occasion when Kevin decided to do the
same assignment as the rest of the class, he wanted to keep doing it for the entire day. Kevin also loved organizing papers. He
would beg me for the chance to collect everyone's completed
work. He would walk around the room, picking up one piece
of paper at a time, placing it carefully in a perfectly aligned
stack. The promise of collecting students' schoolwork became
my only bargaining tool with Kevin. He stayed in his seat many
times simply to get the chance to create neat stacks of paper.

After school, Kevin stayed at the day care center in the
building next to our playground. When I walked from my classroom to the office at the end of each day, I would hear Kevin
call my name. I would turn around and see him waving at me
through the chain link fence. He always seemed to be standing
at the fence. It didn't matter what time I came out of my room,
he was always there, holding on to the fence, waving at me and
calling my name.

One day Kevin got in trouble. I can't remember what he did,
but I moved his chair from his table and placed it in the middle
of the rug at the front of the classroom. By placing him at the
front of the room, close to me, I could make sure he was paying
attention and not bothering the other students sitting at his
table. Simone Roberts, also in trouble, was sitting in a chair
next to him on the rug. This was the first and last time I put students in chairs on the rug as a form of discipline.

I walked back and forth in front of their chairs as I taught the lesson. Suddenly Simone interrupted me. She raised her hand and shouted, "Ms. Sentilles! Ms. Sentilles!"

I said, "Simone, you are already in trouble. I don't need to hear any kind of shouting from you."

"But Ms. Sentilles..."

"Simone, I'm serious. You're interrupting the lesson for everyone. I don't need to hear it."

"But Ms. Sentilles..."

"Cut it out, Simone!"

"But Ms. Sentilles, Kevin tried to smell your butt!"

I was stunned. So was my entire class. I didn't know whether I should laugh or cry. I looked at Kevin. He looked right back at me.

"Is that true, Kevin?" I asked.

"Yeah."

I walked over to my desk, sat down, and slowly wrote a note to Jamie Jones, a third grade teacher at Garvey. My room was silent. Whenever I had a serious problem with a student in my classroom, I sent the student to Jamie's room. This was more to give me a break from the student than to punish the student. The note I wrote to Jamie about Kevin said, "This one tried to smell my butt." I folded the note in half, stapled it shut, chose a student to walk Kevin to Jamie's room, and continued teaching.

When Kevin arrived at Jamie's room, she read the note and thought I was joking. We sometimes amused each other during the school day by writing funny notes back and forth. These notes were our connection to a different world, brief escapes from our classrooms. Thinking the note was a joke, Jamie asked,

"Kevin, what did you do to make Ms. Sentilles send you all the way over here?"

Kevin answered, in a voice loud enough for Jamie's entire class to hear, "I tried to smell my teacher's butt."

"Sweet Jesus!" one of Jamie's students shouted from the back of the room.

Jamie had to leave the room, she was laughing so hard.

Felix Murillo drove me crazy for the first half of the school year. He never followed directions. He always talked to the person sitting next to him when he was supposed to be listening or working. He bothered students at recess. He lied to his mother about his homework. And I always had to tell him everything at least three times.

"Felix, please come to the rug," I would say nicely.

Then a little bit louder, "Felix, please come to the rug and join the rest of the class."

Then I would shout something like, "Felix! Come on! Please pay attention. Everyone is waiting for you."

Then I found out Felix was deaf in one ear. He was deaf in one ear and was just learning English.

Felix's parents found out that he could not hear out of one ear in the middle of the school year. His mother came to see me, practically in tears, clutching an appointment notice from the doctor. I had spent many afternoons talking to her after school about Felix's behavior in the classroom. We knew each other well, or at least we knew how to try to communicate with each other. When I saw her looking so upset, I asked, in Spanish, "What's wrong?"

"Felix cannot hear out of his left ear," she answered. "But the doctor will not give him the operation he needs until summertime."

"Oh, no. I'm so sorry," I said. "Why won't the doctor do the operation now?"

"I don't know. Please call the doctor," she begged me. "Please call the doctor and ask him why he will not do the operation now. Felix's ear is hurting him."

She handed me the appointment notice. I took it, folded it, and put it in the back pocket of the pants I was wearing. "I'll call him," I told her. "I promise I'll call him."

I took the tiny slip of paper home with me that night. I tried to call the number written across the bottom of the page. I sat watching *America's Funniest Home Videos*, eating soup, and listening to the phone ring on the other end of the line. I was exhausted from my day at school. Some days when I came home, I couldn't do anything but open a can of soup, heat it, and sit in front of that stupid television show. The home videos made me laugh. Sometimes they made me laugh so hard I cried.

Teaching in Compton made me so tired that on most days after school I couldn't manage to carry my coffee mug from my car to my apartment. It seemed like it would require too much effort. The floor of the back seat of my car was literally covered in coffee cups, so what good would it do to bring one cup inside? To bring one coffee cup inside, I would have to find the energy to bring the other twenty-five cups inside. So I just left them there.

I tried to call Felix's doctor again the next night, and this time, a woman answered the phone. I gave her my name, the reason I was calling, and a number where the doctor could reach me. He never returned my call. And I never tried to call him again.

Every morning, on my way to the office to get my classroom key, I would see Felix and his mother walking across the campus. Felix would wave at me, and I would wave back. It was our morning ritual. After I found out that Felix could not hear in one ear, I always wondered what his mother thought of me —this teacher who had yelled at and complained about her son for the first four months of school. This teacher who never talked to the doctor about the operation Felix needed. This teacher who struggled to speak Spanish with her and yet was the person who was supposed to be teaching her son how to read in Spanish. I saw Felix every morning at 7:30, and when I saw him, I felt heavy, guilty, ashamed. I saw him, and I was reminded of how many different ways I fell short, missed the mark, failed my students. And the school day had not yet begun.

At the end of each day, I would look around my classroom to see what needed to be done. Sometimes I could do nothing but sit in a small student chair and put my head down, lifting it occasionally to look at the room. I would see the library books that were months overdue. And the special education referral packets stacked in a pile on my desk. And the cabinet I had been meaning to clean out and reorganize since the beginning of the year. And the order forms I never sent home for my students to get student IDs. My feeling at the end of the day was the same feeling I had when I drove in my driveway and couldn't manage to bring my coffee mug inside. Everything seemed too big, too heavy, too hard. I didn't know where to begin. I would think of one thing I needed to do, and then the list would expand infinitely. There was no end. I could only start if I could fix the whole system. Thinking of Felix's ear led to the referral packets, which led to the lessons I needed to plan, which led to the closet to clean, which led to the letters to write, which led to trying to fix the disaster called the Compton Unified School District. I could never see the things I completed, the students I helped, the lessons I taught. I could see only my failures. It was as if I believed the world depended on me. That if I tried harder, was more organized, was better prepared, I could fix it all.

I could not fix it all. I could barely handle my own classroom. I could not even help fix one little boy's ear. Felix reminded me that my students deserved the best—but instead they got me.

CHAPTER III
A DIFFERENT VIOLENCE

THE "YARD" AT Garvey Elementary School was a large expanse of gravel, dirt, cracked asphalt, and broken glass. We had a jungle gym, but all the bars were broken or rusted. We had basketball hoops, but no court, no basketballs, and no nets. We had no kickballs or baseballs or jump ropes. My students invented their own games. Their favorite thing to do was arrange relay races until one day, one of the boys in my class got his leg caught under the broken chain link fence that marked the boundaries of the yard.

At Garvey, my students begged me to let them stay in the classroom during recess. They were willing to do anything— read, clean, nap—in order to avoid having to go outside. In the beginning of the year, when students forgot their homework, I took away their recess. But then many students stopped doing their homework in order to avoid recess. I had to change the consequence. During recess I would peer out my classroom door and see most of my students already lined up next to our classroom number painted on the asphalt. They sat there, quietly talking to each other or reading until the bell rang and they could come back inside.

Teachers didn't like going outside their classrooms either. I dreaded having yard duty—twenty minutes of breaking up fights, standing on hot asphalt in the scorching sun because there was no shade anywhere, and being bombarded by tattle-tales. I ate lunch with another teacher, Jamie Jones, almost every day. I hated walking from my classroom across the yard to her classroom. Students at recess would spot me and run to me, hoping I would be able to solve their problem—a cut knee, a bleeding nose, a punched stomach, a fight over a deflated basketball someone had brought from home. Sometimes I would try to help. Other times I would try to ignore them, running away and waving my arms, shouting, "Talk to the teacher on duty! Talk to the teacher on duty!" They would almost always shout back, exasperated, "We already did."

One afternoon in the spring, the entire second grade at Garvey got in trouble for being "too violent" at recess. The principal gathered all the second graders. We sat in a huge group on the hot asphalt as she yelled at us. "You are too violent," she said. "You need to find another way to play with each other. If you cannot figure out what to do, I will take away recess and make you sit out here for the rest of the year."

Boom. Boom. Boom. Gunshots. All the kids started to scream.

"Stay seated," the principal shouted at us. The teachers ignored her. I organized my class, and we started moving toward our classroom.

"Don't run," the principal shouted.

"Run," I said. "Run."

At All Saints Episcopal Church, the church I attended in Pasadena, a group of parishioners traveled every summer to Aqua Verde, Mexico, to work on the buildings of a school there. After church one Sunday, I looked at the pictures from that summer's trip tacked to a bulletin board. The school in the photographs looked eerily similar to both my schools in Compton. No yard. No grass. Portable buildings. Collapsing ceilings. Peeling paint. Broken fences. An overwhelming sense of gray. Looking at the photographs, I wondered why so many people thought they had to travel to another country to find schools like that to help.

Most people I met in Los Angeles had never been to Compton, even if they had lived in LA their whole lives. "Do you have to wear a bulletproof vest?" they would ask me. The Compton they saw in their heads, like the one I saw in my head before I taught in Compton, had been created by rap lyrics, advertisements, Hollywood, news reports, and television: black men in handcuffs, gang violence, single mothers on welfare, crack addicts.

The Compton I experienced, on the other hand, was a neighborhood of hardworking people struggling to make it, of six- and seven-year-olds and the families who loved them. Compton is violent, but the violence is not like the kind shown on television. Yes, there were drive-by shootings. Yes, I heard gunshots. But these were only the visible symptoms, the consequences of what I came to recognize as the insidious, institutional, intentional violence that permeated the city and its schools, the kind they don't report on the news or portray on television.

The school environments where I worked were violent, and they violated children. Nothing at these schools suggested anything had been invested in the future of these children. From the rabid roaming stray dogs to the lack of shade, the schools were an assaulting and insulting environment. The obvious disrepair of the physical plant of the schools made the oppression experienced by the students seem intentional.

At Garvey Elementary School, I taught over thirty second graders in a so-called temporary building. Most of these "temporary" buildings have been on campuses in Compton for years. The one I taught in was old. Because the wooden beams across the ceiling were being eaten by termites, a fine layer of wood dust covered the students' desks every morning. Maggots crawled in a cracked and collapsing area of the floor near my desk. One day after school I went to sit in my chair, and it was completely covered in maggots. I was nearly sick. Mice raced behind cupboards and bookcases. I trapped six in terrible traps called "glue lounges" given to me by the custodians. The blue metal window coverings on the outsides of the windows were shut permanently, blocking all sunlight. Someone had lost the tool needed to open them, and no one could find another. The air conditioner unit shoved in a hole cut into the back wall of the classroom was so loud we had to turn it off to hear each other.

The fourth and fifth graders at Garvey were housed in a building that had been condemned ten years ago as structurally unsound. The classroom space was needed so desperately that the building was reopened with no structural changes. Four other classes had rooms in portable buildings like mine. The special education program was in a tiny room that smelled so bad that the resource specialist called the Environmental Protection Agency. They boarded up the room and called it a toxic clean-up site. We had no gym. We had no auditorium, no theater, no art rooms, no music rooms, no teachers' lounge, no library.

Jamie Jones hung a sign over the chalkboard in her classroom: "In Room 33, the sky's the limit." In many classrooms in Compton, the sky was, literally, the limit. Ceilings were collapsing all over the district. In one teacher's room at Garvey, the ceiling was in such bad shape that when it rained outside, it rained inside also. Sometimes her room smelled so bad that she could not enter it without feeling sick to her stomach. My first roommate in Los Angeles, Amy Levinson, taught sixth grade at a middle school in Compton. She showed up at school one morning to discover that her entire ceiling had collapsed during the night. In the room where I taught at Garvey, tiles regularly fell from the ceiling. If a tile fell without hitting anyone on the head, my students and I celebrated by ceremonially karate chopping the tile. The tiles were made of a cardboard-like material, and there were four dots of glue on the corners of each tile. I learned at the end of the year, after we had karate chopped at least fifteen tiles, that the four dots were not glue. They were asbestos.

In 1997, at the end of my second year of teaching, the ACLU and Compton parents filed a class action lawsuit against the state superintendent of public instruction for "failure to properly manage Compton Unified School District and provide adequate education and a safe environment" for its students since the state takeover of the district in 1993. The plaintiffs called the victimization of students in Compton schools tantamount to "state-sponsored child abuse."[4] Part of the settlement of the case called for all broken and loose electrical wiring and fixtures to be repaired or replaced; bathrooms to be safe, sanitary, and operable; all schools to remain clean, operational, and free from graffiti; all playground equipment to be repaired or removed if unusable; all broken windows to be replaced; and drinking water to be made available to all children. When interviewed for the documentary film *School Takeover* about the things the state planned to do, Compton mayor Omar Bradley angrily said that these are things one would do for a dog. And yet, incredibly, these were real improvements that needed to be made.

As teachers and students in Compton, we could depend on nothing. Often our classrooms had no electricity. Sometimes we had no water. Once I went to school and discovered someone had broken into our room during the night and had dumped the soil for our garden all over the classroom. Sometimes dismissal was delayed because a man with a gun was hiding from the police on our campus. This violence worked its way into my head, my daily life, so deep down that I even stopped noticing it. It was a vague and throbbing violence, and it was everywhere.

On my first day at Garvey Elementary School, one of the other teachers told me to be careful not to stay in my classroom too long after school. "Why not?" I asked her.

"A woman was raped behind your classroom," she said.

"When?" I asked. "What happened?"

"I really don't know," the teacher told me. "I just heard about it. I heard it happened on the side of the building. There, in that dirt." She pointed at the strip of dirt on the back side of the portable building that was my classroom.

The custodian told me that a man had been shot and killed at Garvey. The dark stain in front of the nurse's office was his blood, he told me. The man who died had been working at Garvey as a substitute custodian. Apparently he was from a different part of Compton, and some people in a gang drove by and saw him. Thinking he was in a rival gang, they opened fire. He ran, and he was shot, and he lay down on the ground in front of the nurse's office, which used to be the principal's office. "He died," the custodian told me. "He died right there. He was only nineteen years old. The principal at that time saw the whole thing. He got in his car, drove away, and never came back."

I don't know if these stories were meant to scare me or to protect me. I don't know if they were true or not. Somehow their truth didn't matter. They were in my head, marking the dirt behind my classroom, staining the cement in front of the nurse's office, circumscribing the space of my days, interrupting my lessons.

One afternoon, Mrs. Carson, the principal of Garvey Elementary School, knocked on my door in the middle of a math lesson. "Ms. Sentilles, we need you to translate for the police," she told me. I left my classroom full of children, and we walked across the yard and out the metal gate. Two policemen and a vendor were standing in the middle of the street. I had seen the vendor before. He had a little cart on wheels and sold ice cream to kids after school.

"Do you speak Spanish?" one of the policemen asked me. "Yes," I said.

"Then translate this to this asshole. You tell him if I hear about or see him touching little girls again, or if I see him anywhere near this school again, I will kick his fucking ass."

I turned to look at the man these police were accusing of touching little girls. He looked terrified. I introduced myself, and then he started talking, telling me he did not know what they were saying, that he had done nothing wrong. I told him they said he was bothering girls. He said he had never done anything like that. He just sold ice cream, trying to make some money for his family.

"What are you telling him?" the policeman asked me.

"He says he didn't do anything," I said.

"Tell him what I told you to tell him. Tell him if I see him here again, I will kick his fucking ass. Tell him that."

"I don't know how to say that in Spanish," I said. "I don't know the words for 'kick your fucking ass.'"

Despite the high incidence of shootings in the neighborhoods surrounding both schools where I worked in Compton, we did not have a security guard or an intercom system. To communicate messages to different classrooms, students were sent as "runners" from the office. The runners would knock on the designated classroom's door to deliver the message. One teacher's class kept a tally of the number of interruptions that happened in their classroom before 10:00 in the morning. The record number was nineteen. If there was a violent emergency—a shooting in the neighborhood, a police chase on campus—the runner would dart from classroom to classroom, knocking on each door and shouting "Code Yellow." Teachers were then to lock the door and instruct their students to sit on the floor. No one was allowed to leave the classroom. No one was to answer the door for any reason.

One afternoon at Garvey, I lined up my students to be dismissed, opened the door, and let my class out in two lines. Mrs. Wallace, the assistant principal, was standing outside my classroom, holding a clipboard and a walkie-talkie. As the two lines of students filed out of the classroom, Mrs. Wallace said, "Ms. Sentilles, you need to bring your class back inside."

It had been a difficult day with my students. I had let them out two minutes early. I thought she was being picky. I was annoyed. "It's almost 2:15, Mrs. Wallace. It's time to go home," I said.

"Ms. Sentilles, you need to bring your class back inside."

I rolled my eyes.

"Ms. Sentilles, there has been a shooting."

"Oh." I looked around at the rest of the campus. No other classes were lined up to go home. I hadn't heard any gunshots. No one had knocked on my door to inform me of the "Code Yellow." I had almost dismissed my students into gunfire.

The occasional gunfire that punctuated my teaching experience in Compton, although terrifying and horrific, was minor compared to the daily violence of the school environment itself. Poverty is violent. In this chapter, you will meet just a few of the many students who attended the bare, unprotected, hostile schools of Compton. Again and again, my students responded to the violence of their environment with hope, love, and incredible resilience. I didn't always behave so gracefully. I discovered a rage in myself that made me afraid.

✑ ✑ ✑

Max Davis unearthed his love for plants in my first grade class. His father's name was Miles Davis. Because of his father's name, I liked Max immediately.

The day after I taught my students about seeds, about what seeds need to grow into plants, Mr. Davis came to school with Max, who was carrying a glass jar filled with dirt. When Max saw me, he hid behind his father. Mr. Davis said, "Go ahead, son, ask her."

Max shook his head.

"Come on, Max," Mr. Davis said again. "Ask her."

Max shook his head harder and hid further behind his father.

"Max, I brought this to school so you could ask her. You see, Ms. Sentilles, we are having a little discussion about seeds— aren't we, Max?"

"Yes," said Max. He took a deep breath. "Ms. Sentilles, you said that if I planted a sunflower seed it would grow into a sunflower."

"That's right. It will," I said.

"Well, I planted a sunflower seed, and look, it hasn't grown at all," Max said as he thrust the glass jar filled with dirt up toward my face.

"Max," I asked. "When did you plant the seed?"

"Yesterday!" he shouted, as if that was the most obvious thing in the world.

"I guess I should have been more specific in class, Max. Seeds need soil, sun, water, love—and time."

"See," Mr. Davis said as he winked at me. "I told you it would grow. It just needs a little time." Max handed the jar back to his dad and hugged him. Then he took my hand and followed me into the classroom.

Throughout my first year as a teacher at Madison, my friends from college came to visit me in Los Angeles. They came to see me teach. My students were always as excited to see my friends as I was. They loved all visitors immediately. The day before we were to have a visitor, I would tell them the name of my friend who was coming to see them. The next morning, each one would run up to the visiting person and hug her, shouting, "Welcome to Madison! I'm glad to see you!"

One of my roommates from Yale, Anne Guerry, came with me one morning to Madison. I took her to the yard where I greeted and picked up my students. The morning was my favorite part of the day. It was filled with hope and promise. I also had the chance to visit with parents. I spoke with some in Spanish and some in English.

On the Monday Anne visited, my students arrived carrying different types of food. The homework assignment from the Friday before was to bring a piece of food from one of the four food groups. I saw Max and Mr. Davis walking to the line. Mr. Davis was carrying an enormous watermelon.

"Sarah," he said. "Can I talk to you for a second?"

"Sure, Mr. Davis. What can I do for you?"

"Max wanted to bring a watermelon to school today."

"That's great. What a good idea."

"So, it's OK that he brought a watermelon?"

"Sure. I think it's wonderful, as long as he knows which food group it belongs to."

"Oh, he knows," Mr. Davis said. "I hope you don't mind carrying it." Mr. Davis handed me the watermelon, and Max stood in line with the rest of the class.

I looked at my friend Anne. She was crying. "Anne," I whispered. "What's wrong? You can't cry in the morning. Nothing traumatic has happened yet." She turned and walked to the end of the line so my students couldn't see her face.

Because it was Monday, we had to say the Pledge of Allegiance in English and Spanish as an entire school. I knew that if Anne was already crying, she was going to cry harder during the Pledge. The flag we faced during the Pledge was painted on the side of a classroom building, painted to look like it was waving in the wind. To the right of the flag were three larger-than-life smiling children's faces. It was hard to make out exactly what was written on the mural because graffiti covered so much of it, but I think the words painted below these faces once said, "We are winners" in big white letters. Parts of the faces, the stars on the flag, and the blue background had been marked—*tagged*, it was called in Compton—by various groups claiming this wall as their own. Patches of color that didn't match the color of the original mural tried to hide the graffiti. The mural had been fixed so many times it resembled a patchwork quilt. The newest additions to the mural were three large fluorescent splatters from a paintball gun. Melanie, a student in my class, whispered to me at recess one day that her dad had made those marks on the wall in the middle of the night. Whoever had been trying to preserve the mural had given up long ago. Graffiti reigned. This was our American flag, the wall we faced every Monday morning to say in clear, loud voices, "One nation, under God, with liberty and justice for all."

My first grade class and I planted a garden. I covered a patch of grass outside our classroom with soil and lined it with short stakes and string. We planted cilantro, carrots, nasturtiums, beans, parsley, mint, and (for Max) sunflowers. We took good care of our garden. We watered it. We weeded it. We charted the growth of each type of plant. In the mornings, I would find students' mothers picking cilantro to use in their cooking. The garden was beautiful, and we were all very proud of it.

When I first told the principal, Mrs. Redding, that I wanted to plant a garden, she laughed at me and said, "It will be destroyed and vandalized before anything has a chance to grow." Almost every other teacher expressed my principal's opinion when they saw me unloading the soil from my car and dumping it on the grass in front of my classroom. They thought I was wasting my time and money. But I decided to plant the garden anyway. I trusted the students and the neighborhood to respect the garden. I believed the reason our school was vandalized was because it was so ugly. I thought the vandals were meeting disrespect with disrespect. The garden, I hoped, would be beautiful, and so people would leave it alone.

And they did. Students—both from my classroom and from other classrooms—guarded our garden during recess. They begged me to let them water it all the time. Parents helped weed it in the morning. Students brought rulers from home to measure the plants' progress. The garden grew and grew. When the sunflowers were taller than my first graders, I took Polaroid pictures of them standing in front of the gigantic flowers.

The day after I took the photographs, I arrived at Madison to discover the garden had been destroyed. The sunflowers were slashed, their big stalks cut in half or ripped into several pieces. Bicycle tires had ripped up the soil and any small plants in their way. The cilantro was gone. The carrots were pulled out of the ground. The garden was ruined. I started to cry. Mrs. Redding saw me kneeling on the grass near the destroyed garden, and she said, "Well, Ms. Sentilles, I guess this is a teachable moment." And then she walked away. I wondered what she meant, what she could have possibly thought my students were supposed to learn.

My students began to arrive at school. They gathered silently around our destroyed garden. I didn't know what to say or how to handle the situation. We stood and looked at the garden for a long time, and then we moved into the classroom. When everyone was inside the room, I asked, "How did seeing the garden make you feel?" They answered: sad, angry, disappointed, hurt, confused. Then I asked, "How do you think the people who ruined the garden were feeling when they destroyed it?" Almost every student said something like, "Whoever did that to our garden must have been very sad and very angry." We talked about what it felt like to have someone ruin something that was important to us, and to remember that feeling so we would not ever purposefully hurt someone or something that belonged to someone else.

Then I took my first graders outside, and we held hands as we slowly danced around our ruined garden in a silent circle.

When we went back inside, we talked about what kinds of plants we would put in our new garden. We decided to call our next garden "The Victory Garden." The following day, Max brought a packet of sunflower seeds for the Victory Garden. He said, "Here you go, Ms. Sentilles. They'll grow again real soon."

Asha Rose was a tiny girl with an enormous father who helped repair our garden after it was destroyed. He was extremely tall and had the largest hands I have ever seen. His head was shaved so closely that from a distance he appeared to be bald. He loved his family and was as gentle and soft spoken as he was big.

He brought Asha to school fifteen minutes late almost every day. He would walk quietly through the open door at the back of my first grade classroom holding Asha's hand. They would hug, and she would walk to the rug to join the rest of the class as we did our morning routine. Her father would watch us for a few minutes, wave at me, smile, and then walk out of the room.

Asha's mother was beautiful. She picked Asha and her little brother up after school every day. We talked about Asha's progress and behavior. I loved their family. I loved the way they loved each other. I loved how the mother and father shared the task of raising their children. But I knew nothing about them, really, and as I fell in love with the family I wrote their story in my mind. I imagined their family dinners, their time together on the weekends. I felt I knew them and understood them.

One day, my students and I somehow started to talk about guns. I asked my first graders if they had ever seen anyone get shot. All of them—every single person in the room except me—raised their hands. I looked at my students, my six- and seven-year-old students, raising their hands as they sat on a multicolored carpet covered with shapes and the letters of the alphabet. All of my students put their hands down, except for Asha. She kept hers raised.

"Yes, Asha?" I asked.

"I saw someone get shot last night."

"What happened?" I asked.

"Well, I didn't exactly see it. I heard it. They shot my cousin in the head last night. She died. They live right below us."

The room erupted into shooting stories, but I didn't—or couldn't—hear them. I caught bits and pieces of uncles and cousins and neighbors being shot, of people dying in driveways and bedrooms and living rooms. I heard about car doors slamming, heads jerking back, and broken bodies falling to the floor. I looked at Asha, and when the room quieted down, I said, "How do you feel, Asha? Are you OK?"

She just looked at me and shrugged, lifting her tiny shoulders to her ears and letting them fall again. She was sitting on her knees. I didn't know what to say. I started teaching a new math lesson on subtraction.

After our garden was destroyed, I found Asha's father trying to put the garden back together again. He was on his hands and knees surrounded by pieces of wood and rolls of string and a hammer. I was on my way back from taking my students to recess when I saw him. "Mr. Rose," I said. "What are you doing?"

"I'm trying to fix your garden," he said. He had already replanted the uprooted carrots. He said, "I heard all the teachers and parents telling you how sorry they were about your garden, but they weren't helping you. I felt bad for you, so I thought I would try to help."

"Thank you so much," I said, moved by his kindness.

"No problem. I'm glad to do it."

"I have been meaning to tell you what a beautiful family you have," I said, standing next to him as he worked to repair the sunflowers.

"Thank you. I think so, too."

"I really love your family. I love to see you all together."

"I love to see us together, too. I missed them."

"What do you mean?" I asked.

"Well," he said slowly. "I was in prison for a while and I just got out, and so I am happy to be able to be back with my family."

"Oh," I said, stunned.

"I was crazy then. I was on drugs and my mind was crazy. I found God, though. I'm a new man now," he said.

I didn't know what to say, so I stayed quiet. I watched as he worked. He carefully straightened the broken sunflower stems. He used white string to tie the wooden stakes to the lower half of the stalks, strengthening the sunflowers so they could stand again.

✎ ✎ ✎

Even after Asha told us she had seen her cousin shot and killed, even after everyone in my classroom admitted to having seen someone get shot, I didn't think I would ever actually see someone shot. At that point I had never even heard gunfire. Then one afternoon a few weeks later, while I was still at school after the school day had ended, there was a drive-by shooting down the street from Madison.

This happened just after Eliot Carleton's mother had been visiting my classroom. Eliot was my first favorite student. I wanted to be his favorite teacher. I even worried that Eliot would get mad at me, so I changed my behavior for him in the classroom: I called on him more than I should have, I let him be line leader when it was not really his turn. I took Eliot to various places around Los Angeles. We visited the Los Angeles Museum of Art and the La Brea Tar Pits. We drove to LAX to watch planes take off. We ate ice cream. We picked out my cat from the humane society. It was strange that as a twenty-one-year-old I worried about the opinion of a six-year-old, but I did. This was before I realized that I needed six-year-old students, not six-year-old friends. But Eliot was my friend, and his mother was my hero.

Eliot dressed up for school every day—long pants, long-sleeved shirt, fancy shoes. He had school clothes and regular clothes. There was officially no school on days when we had parent-teacher conferences, so Eliot accompanied his mother to the conferences in his regular clothes: tank top or T-shirt and shorts.

Once I dropped by the Carletons' house, a blue house on the corner of Walter Avenue, unannounced. Mrs. Carleton answered the door and gave me a big hug. We sat at her din-ing room table and talked, surrounded by photographs of her children and grandchildren. Eliot was her baby; her older chil-dren already had children of their own. She was simultaneously mother and grandmother. Mrs. Carleton had been sewing when I arrived. She told me she sewed clothing to make extra money. While we were talking, I heard drums in the background.

"Who's playing the drums?" I asked.

"That's Eliot," she said.

"Eliot plays the drums?"

"He loves the drums," she said. "I thought you knew that. Let's go see him. You have to be real quiet, though, because he'll stop playing if he hears you."

We tiptoed to the back of the house, to the small room that was Eliot's. Eliot was sitting on an upside-down bucket, wear-ing a pair of shorts and no shirt. His drum set was homemade: a collection of different-sized buckets organized in a semicir-cle around the bucket he was sitting on. He was playing hard, sweating and moving his head up and down. "I want to get him a real set," his mother whispered to me, "but I haven't been able to afford it yet."

We listened for a long time before Eliot realized we were there. Then he saw me and stopped, embarrassed, not so much because he had been playing the drums, I think, but because he was not wearing a shirt. "Oh, Ms. Sentilles!" he said as he ran to the chest of drawers and grabbed a shirt. "When did you get here?"

Two weeks after I heard Eliot play the drums, he refused to go to recess. While the other students were outside, I sat in the classroom with him and tried to find out what was wrong. I don't remember what I said to him, but I remember what he said to me. When he grew up, he told me, he was going to kill himself. He wanted to be with his Nana, he said, and he was always getting into trouble anyway.

I immediately called Eliot's mother and asked her to come to school. She came to see me at the end of the school day. When Mrs. Carleton arrived, we sat at the low, long table at the back of my classroom, each of us in a small student chair. Together we tried to understand what would make Eliot say he wanted to kill himself when he grew up, what would make him want to be dead. We sat close to each other, our knees almost touching. We whispered because Eliot was playing near us on the classroom's carpet. Mrs. Carleton told me she was not going to let this child slip by her. She had missed, somehow, with her other two children. She spoke of her struggles as a mother trying to raise three children on her own. When Eliot's father—the muscled man he always drew in his pictures—left, she tried to stay home to raise her children. But welfare didn't provide enough money for them to live, so she returned to work. She believed her two older children's grades had slipped in school because she was never around to help them with their homework or to go to their schools because she was always at work. When Eliot was old enough to go to school, Mrs. Carleton started to work at night so she could come to school with Eliot during the day. She volunteered at every school event. She worked with the PTA. She visited my classroom daily. I don't know when she found time to sleep.

When we finished talking, she closed her small suitcase containing the Mother's Day cards she was selling to raise money for the PTA. She called to Eliot, took his hand, and walked out of my room.

I sat back down at the table and started to make index cards for the next day's lesson on subject-verb agreement. Mrs. Redding was going to observe me the following day to evaluate my teaching. I wrote the nouns in red and the verbs in blue. Cat. Cats. Power Ranger. Power Rangers. Teacher. Teachers. Grow. Grows. Eat. Eats. Is. Are.

Ta-ta-ta-do-do-do-ta-tatatatatatatatatatatatatatatata

It took several seconds for me to place the sound, to label it "gunfire," to realize someone was shooting. Then I hit the floor. I remember being aware of the grit on the tile floor, studying the dirt trapped in the thin lines between each beige square that made up the floor of my classroom. I heard round after round of gunfire. Automatic gunfire. I had never heard this before. I had never even heard a single gunshot before. Suddenly there was silence.

I got up off the floor, closed the doors of my classroom, which had been open to create a cross-breeze, and started to make index cards again. Flower. Flowers. Bloom. Blooms.

Faith Tyler, a fourth grade teacher at Madison, ran into my room. "Sarah!" she shouted, "What are you doing? We've got to get out of here!"

"I'm getting evaluated tomorrow. I have to finish getting my room and my lesson ready," I said.

"Who cares? Let's go! Let's go! Come on. We have to go."

I grabbed my things. There wasn't time to put on my shoes. Faith and I ran to the parking lot, joining the stream of other running teachers. I climbed, barefoot, into my car, started the engine, and pulled out of the fenced parking lot, passing a police car with flashing lights but no siren. I looked down Riverdale Avenue, the street I drove up every morning on my way to school. It was already blocked off with yellow police tape, but I couldn't see what was happening. I drove away. I drove and drove, in a daze, not really seeing anything until I stopped in front of the house where I lived in Hollywood.

I sat on my front steps, drinking a beer and thinking about Eliot. During the shooting, Mrs. Carleton and Eliot must have been walking toward their house to eat dinner together. Mrs. Carleton had just learned her son, her baby, her six-year-old, wanted to kill himself. What were they talking about when they heard those shots?

Semiautomatic gunfire had followed Eliot and his mother home, but on the evening news, nothing. I read the paper the next morning. Nothing. No mention of the events on Riverdale Avenue in front of Madison Elementary School at 4:15 in the afternoon. The whole thing was erased as if it had never existed.

Riverdale Avenue erased it, too. The next afternoon as I drove out of the parking lot after a full day of teaching—this time wearing shoes—I looked down Riverdale Avenue to see if I could see evidence of the shooting. I expected police tape, cars riddled with bullet holes, armed guards. But it looked like it had looked every day before the shooting. The tricycles were back, the ice cream truck was still playing "It's a Small World, After All," and people were sitting on their stoops again.

Two men were killed by the gunfire I heard that day. For the rest of the week following the shootings, after I dropped off my students at recess or lunch, I would walk along the chain link fence separating Madison Elementary School from Riverdale Avenue and wonder if there would be more shootings. What it meant to have a good day at school changed also. I would come home and say to my roommate, "It was a good day. No bullets." We would both laugh.

I was often lonely during my time as a teacher in Compton, but I was the loneliest during the week right after the shooting. I felt lonely when I spoke to my parents. I couldn't tell them about it because I didn't want them to worry about me any more than they already did. I felt lonely around my friends. I couldn't tell them about the shooting because I felt that if I told people I had been at school during a drive-by shooting, I would be contributing to Compton's dismal reputation, fueling the fears that kept people away from places like Compton, as if just pulling off the highway put them in danger. And I felt lonely at school. Unlike my students, I got to leave Compton every day after school. I went home, sat on my front steps, and felt safe. My kids spent every night in Compton. They heard gunfire and police helicopters on many occasions. It was their school, their street, their city. I was just a visitor.

My roommate in Venice Beach, Yuki Murata, visited my classroom at Garvey several times. On her first visit, she asked to use the restroom. I pointed her in the direction of the faculty restroom, but she found only the student restroom. She came back and said, "Sarah, there were no doors on the stalls. There was no toilet paper. There were no paper towels or soap. It smelled horrible. Do the students actually use that bathroom?"

Later that day, a group of girls ran up to me on the playground. "Carolina went to the bathroom on the slide!" they shouted.

"What?" I asked, not understanding.

"Carolina Uribe went to the bathroom on the playground."

I ran to the slide. Carolina was sitting on the sand at the bottom, crying, a wet circle all around her. During recess someone had locked all the student bathrooms, and so there was nowhere for her to go. She couldn't hold it any longer, and so she had an accident on the playground in front of all her friends and classmates.

I brought Carolina to the office so she could call her parents for some clean clothes. I asked the principal why the bathrooms were locked. She told me students had been throwing water at each other and shouting. Boys were urinating on the walls.

"Well," I said, "now people are urinating on the playground."

I am still surprised when I use a public restroom and it has toilet seat covers, toilet paper, soap, and paper towels. In faculty restrooms in Compton, it was a good day if I found one of the four items. On my way to the bathroom, I sometimes tried to guess what I would find. Would it be toilet paper? Or soap? In the student restrooms, there was nothing. No paper of any kind. No soap. And definitely no toilet seat covers. Sometimes there weren't even any toilet seats. I once heard someone on the faculty say about Garvey, "If this were a prison, it would be shut down."

✎ ✎ ✎

When Eva Hernandez first joined my class, she spent most of her recess time hiding in the bathroom. She had nervous eyes. They seemed to vibrate with anxiety, looking side to side in quick, jerky motions. Her head, too, moved from side to side, seemingly driven by the movement of her eyes. Her neck always looked tense, as if she were desperately trying to keep her head still, but the terror behind her eyes proved stronger.

She arrived at the door of my second grade classroom halfway through the year. Like so many students who enrolled after school had already started, Eva appeared with no academic records, no notes about where she had been in school before, no information other than the fact that she had been sent from the office at Garvey to my classroom. I wondered where she had been before she appeared at my door. Even more, I wondered what she had seen.

I had trouble with Eva in the classroom, not because of how she herself behaved, but because of the other girls she chose as her friends, two difficult girls named Sandra and Loretta. Soon after Eva's arrival, the three girls developed a habit of coming in late from recess. At the end of recess, I would line up my class and walk them slowly toward our classroom door. Whenever we came back to the classroom from being out on the yard, each member of our class entered one at a time. I shook every student's hand, welcoming him or her by name back to the room. Most students shook my hand, giggled, and then gave me a big hug. Even though this hand-shaking welcome took several minutes, Loretta, Eva, and Sandra would still have not appeared before I closed the door to begin teaching again.

I decided to call home to let the parents know their children were spending class time wandering around an unsafe campus. When I called Eva's mother, she said she would come see me the next day.

At the end of the day, there was a knock on my door. I opened it. A woman in short spandex shorts and a loose white tank top stood on the steps to my classroom with her hands on her hips. Her hair seemed to have been bleached with peroxide, and it stuck out in clumps on her head. She wore black eye makeup, and her eyeliner was smeared below her eyes. She had no eyebrows, but she had penciled in replacements in high arches in the middle of her forehead.

"Eva!" she shouted.

I turned around to find her. Eva raised herself from her seat. Her anxiety was palpable. She began to walk, slowly, toward the open door. When she reached the door, her mother stretched a long arm into the classroom, grabbed Eva, and dragged her out onto the steps. I then watched as her mother lifted her arm high in the air and brought it down quickly and slapped Eva's face. The sound of it echoed. Eva's cheek reddened immediately.

"It won't happen again," her mother shouted at me. Then she turned, taking Eva with her, and slammed the door. Our room was silent, still, stunned. I turned to look at my students. They looked at me with wide eyes. I believe they felt betrayed.

I knew then both that they trusted me and that I had betrayed that trust. I was the teacher, the adult in the room. I was supposed to keep them safe, from bullies on the playground, from the stray wandering dogs on the yard, from gunmen who hid on our campus—even, sometimes, from the people in their lives who were supposed to love them. Eva's mother stood in the doorway of our classroom and brutally slapped her seven-year-old daughter. And I had done nothing but stand there and watch.

I have replayed that scene in my mind again and again. Each time the events unfold as if in slow motion, but still, like a recurring nightmare whose ending I know, I can't stop her mother's arm from slapping her face. I *can't* stop her mother, or I *don't*? It is this confusion, this regret, this shame that has wrapped itself in a tight ball that lives in the middle of my chest, sometimes making it hard to breathe.

I was not the only one who had trouble breathing in Compton. Many children in Compton have asthma. Martin Villareal, a third grader in Jamie Jones's classroom, had asthma. He was also constantly in trouble. When Jamie needed time out from him, she sent him to my room. I took a different approach with Martin than I did with the other students who were sent to my room. Instead of ostracizing him, forcing him to sit in the corner and do extra schoolwork, I had him participate in my classroom activities. He became my helper. In his third grade classroom, Martin needed extra help with almost every assignment. In my second grade classroom, he was the expert, kind and patient, helping my students with math, reading, and art. Martin thrived in this leadership role. Eventually Jamie and I decided we could use my classroom as a reward rather than as a punishment for Martin. Every morning, Martin would find me and ask if he could come and help me in my room. We would make a deal—if he did all his morning schoolwork, he could help my class in the afternoon.

On Valentine's Day, Martin made a valentine for me that said, "Dear Ms. Sentilles, I give this heart to you because I love your class. You are my best friends. Love, Mr. Martin." My students loved Martin as much as he loved them. When he came to help our class, he would position himself next to whichever student he had determined might need a little extra help. He was bilingual, so he often chose students who struggled with English. He even played with my class, rather than with his own, during recess. Martin's favorite student was Marcus Martinez. During one lesson on Salvador Dalí, Martin helped Marcus create a surrealist collage. Using several magazines, the two boys created a masterpiece, including images of human bodies with clocks for heads.

One of my favorite second grade lessons was the one for compound words. Jamie's third grade class discovered my love for compound words, and her students would find me throughout the day to share ones they had discovered. Martin found me during one morning recess and said, "Ms. Sentilles, I have a compound word for you: 'wheelchair.' "

"That's great, Martin," I said. "What are the two words in 'wheelchair'?"

" 'Wheel' and 'chair,' " he said.

"Perfect. How did you think of that word?"

"I made someone be in a wheelchair," he said.

I didn't understand. "What do you mean, Martin?" I asked.

"I play ice hockey, and this boy was hitting me and pushing me and so I hit him really, really hard with my stick, and now he can't walk anymore. He's in a wheelchair."

Martin narrated the event to me in a very matter-of-fact tone of voice, the same tone he used to tell me "wheelchair" was a compound word. I was stunned. Seven-year-old Martin hit another little boy so hard with an ice hockey stick that the boy lost his ability to walk. "Oh, Martin," I said. "When did this happen?"

"Last week during my game."

"How do you feel?"

"I feel bad. I said I was sorry I hit him. But I am not allowed to play hockey anymore."

"Have you talked to anyone about what happened?"

"No. I didn't talk to anyone about it."

"I'll talk to Ms. Jones and see if we can find someone for you to talk to. If you need to talk about it, come find me, OK?"

"Yeah, OK. I will," Martin said.

I looked at Martin, at his long, dark eyelashes, his carefully combed hair, his blue and white school uniform. Martin's eyes had always seemed haunted to me. They could change in an instant. Calm one minute, full of rage the next. The rage seemed to lie in wait at the back of his eyes. It was this rage that drove

Jamie to send him to my classroom. This rage made Martin unpredictable, dangerous. Jamie never knew if he would respond with tears or fists. I thought I could overcome Martin's rage, could calm him, help him find peace, simply by giving him responsibility in my classroom, as if being a line leader would make a difference.

I looked at Martin, pictured him skating on the ice. I imagined the boy who had bothered him, bullied him, pushed him. And I imagined something clicking inside Martin's head, something breaking. He had had enough. And he lashed out at the boy. He hit him, and then he hit him again. Again and again, until the boy was broken and couldn't walk anymore.

What frightened me most was not the image, but the fact that I could relate to Martin. Teaching in Compton, I had discovered anger inside me deeper and wilder than any emotion I had experienced before. I could imagine myself skating on that ice and becoming sick and tired of getting beat up. I could feel that rage boiling inside me, overflowing, uncontainable, and coming out in swift, violent motions of *my* hockey stick. *This* is for the missing textbooks. *This* is for not letting me use the copy machine. *This* is for the man who opened fire during our Halloween carnival. *This* is for all the people who ever asked me if I have to wear a bulletproof vest when I'm teaching. *This* is for my students.

"Can I come help you in your classroom this afternoon?" Martin asked, pulling me out of my reverie.

"Sure," I said. "I'll tell Ms. Jones."

Martin smiled, turned, and ran toward the rusted monkey bars and broken fences to join his friends at recess.

Moses Reyes, one of Martin's third grade classmates, loved compound words as much as I did. Sometimes we would speak to each other only in compound words—baseball, playground, undercover, sidewalk.

During one morning recess when I was standing on the yard with Jamie, Moses asked us a question. "Can someone fire God?"

Jamie and I looked at each other, startled, and then responded, "We don't know. What do you think?"

Moses put one finger under his chin and looked up, his head tilted back and a little to the left. "Yeah, I think so," he said. "I think someone could fire God if God did something bad instead of good like He is supposed to. Then I think God might get fired."

He visited me in my classroom that same afternoon after school. "I have another question, Ms. Sentilles," he said.

"Yes, Moses?"

"Does anything else know it's going to die?"

"What do you mean, Moses?" I looked at this little boy standing in front of me, wearing the school uniform of blue pants and a white button-down shirt and asking me about death. Although it was the end of the day, his hair was still perfectly combed and his shirt was carefully tucked into his pants. I hoped I had misunderstood his question.

"I mean," Moses explained, "do you think we are the only things that know we are going to die or do you think birds or other animals know?"

"I'm not sure," I said. "What do you think?"

"I think," said Moses, "they don't know. Otherwise they'd be more careful."

✎ ✎ ✎

Elise and Olivia Carter were sisters in my second grade class. I'm not sure who was older. Both were born addicted to drugs.

Elise was extremely thin and small. She had skinny arms and skinny legs. Her fingers were long and bony. Her head was small in relation to her body. Elise moved constantly, and she always had something in her mouth—fingers, schoolwork, crayons, pencils, papers, or anything else she could find. When she sat in her seat, she rocked from side to side and sucked on her fingers. As she rocked, she moved her head back and forth, back and forth, as if she were tracing an infinity sign with her chin. Her hair was usually braided with extensions. On the end of each braid were several plastic beads. Sometimes the beads were white, sometimes they were different colors, but they always made noise, clicking together in rhythm to the swinging of her head. Elise needed to move so much that I taped a line of masking tape on the floor in the back of my room. My class called it Elise's Line. When Elise felt she could not sit in her seat for another second, she was allowed to get up and go to the line. There, in the back of the room, she spent time walking back and forth, up and down the line.

Olivia was the physical and behavioral opposite of her sister. While Elise was thin and bony, Olivia was solid, her fingers as short as Elise's were long. While Elise ran everywhere, Olivia walked slowly and deliberately. Olivia was calm, almost eerily calm, and she was the only person who could calm her sister down. Olivia would walk to wherever Elise was and put her thick arm around Elise's bony shoulders. Elise would immediately stop rocking and lean quietly against her sister. Olivia was easy to have in the classroom because she was so quiet that she almost disappeared, raising her voice only to say an occasional "Elise!" when Elise was being particularly disruptive. But Olivia's mind was slower than Elise's. Elise could grasp new concepts easily, but her inability to sit still meant that she couldn't focus on a lesson or complete her work. Olivia could sit still, and she could concentrate on her schoolwork, but her mind had trouble with concepts. In the classroom, Olivia appeared to be doing her work. I would watch her as she sat at her desk working—her head bent low while she concentrated on the assignment. Then fifteen minutes later, while the rest of the class was finishing their work, I would walk to her desk, look down at her paper, and realize she had spent the entire time writing her name in careful, perfect letters across the top of the page.

Elise and Olivia's mother was no longer addicted to drugs, but she was sick. She was suffering from a kidney problem, I think, but I was never quite sure. I was also not sure exactly who lived in their house, but judging from who answered the phone when I called, I gathered they lived with their mother, an aunt, a grandmother, and some cousins. When their mother was especially sick, in bed or in the hospital, Elise and Olivia would come to school looking very sad. They would ask me if they could have some extra time to make cards for her. I always let them, and they would create beautiful cards filled with rainbows and balloons and hearts. Sometimes Elise and Olivia didn't come to school because their mother was so sick. I would find their cousin, who was also in second grade, and ask her where they were. "They had to take care of their mom," the cousin would say.

"What do you mean?" I would ask.

"You know, they had to cook her breakfast and spend time with her by the bed."

In the beginning of the school year, Elise participated in the Resource Specialist Program (RSP), Compton's version of a program for students with special needs. She spent one hour each afternoon working with Mrs. Kay, the resource specialist. Elise looked forward to her time with Mrs. Kay and so did I. The classroom was noticeably different without Elise in it. When she left to spend her hour in RSP, a calm would descend on our room. Elise's constant movements and interruptions made the entire class feel frantic; when she was gone things seemed still. Elise, too, was transformed by her time with Mrs. Kay. She thrived on the extra attention, and her behavior and performance in the classroom dramatically improved. I called Elise's mother occasionally to talk to her about Elise. During one phone call in early November, a few weeks into Elise's time with Mrs. Kay, Elise's mother could not stop thanking me for the progress Elise was making at home and in school. I could not take credit for the improvement, I told her. Most of the credit belonged to Mrs. Kay.

Later that same November, I received a notice in my staff mailbox stating that due to a lack of students enrolled in RSP at Garvey, Mrs. Kay would be dividing her time between Garvey and another elementary school in Compton. Elise's time with Mrs. Kay, this notice said, would be reduced from five days a week to one day a week: Mondays, 1:00 to 2:00 in the afternoon. That was it.

"A lack of students?" I thought as I read the memo. In my classroom alone, I had referred seven students to RSP, and I knew of a long list of students from other classrooms waiting to get into the program. The only reason Elise was in RSP and these other students were not was that Elise's first grade teacher had referred her to RSP at the beginning of the previous school year. The paperwork had taken over a year to process. At Garvey, the referral process took so long that by the end of the school year, none of the second grade students I referred to RSP had even been tested, the first stage of the process.

A regular classroom—by regular, I mean a Compton Unified School District classroom, a classroom filled with over thirty students and one teacher—did not meet Elise's educational needs. It also detracted from the education of every other student in my room. Elise demanded most of my attention. I always had to watch her, calm her, ask her to sit in her seat, make sure she was not eating something toxic, ask her to stop talking, put my hand on her shoulder so she would stop rocking and swinging her beads, tell her to stop pointing her middle finger at other students. Because the school was not providing an appropriate education for Elise, her mother tried to have the state provide help for her. I filled out form after form. One of the forms asked me if I thought Elise's mother was exaggerating Elise's problem to get extra money. I wrote a big "NO" in that space.

Elise was never enrolled in a different program. She stayed with me for the entire school year. Sometimes I seemed to have an endless supply of patience and energy for her. Other times I had nothing left to give.

One day, I reached a breaking point with her. Elise had wandered around the room or eaten a crayon or swung her head or opened her mouth or disrupted a lesson or not followed directions or come late from recess one too many times. Something in me snapped. I looked at her, and all I felt was rage. I was ready to hit, scream, grab, throw. I was ready to hurt someone. Before I knew what I was doing, I grabbed Elise by her wrist, hard. I pulled her to the door, opened it, and practically threw her out of the classroom. I pushed her out the door, still holding on to her wrist, her tiny, tiny wrist, and forced her down the three stairs leading to my portable classroom. She stumbled and almost fell, and in that instant, watching her struggle to keep her balance against the force of my angry grip, I saw her. I saw myself. I realized how close to abusing her I had come. I let go of her wrist. She looked at me and started to cry, hiding her face in her hands and leaning against the wall of the building. I quietly asked her to please go back inside the room. She did. I closed the door and stayed outside, alone. I sat on the steps, surrounded by the voices of children, and I held my head in my hands and wept.

CHAPTER IV

WHAT WE NEED

AT GARVEY, we had everything we needed to have a library. We had a room. We had shelves. We had books. And we had a paid librarian. But no students were allowed to use the library—not to check out books, not for classroom visits, not to listen to the librarian read a story. Instead, we used the library for our faculty meetings on Monday afternoons after school. Sitting through these meetings, surrounded by books no one ever read, epitomized teaching in Compton: the pieces seemed to be there, but nothing worked quite the way it was supposed to.

I spent thousands of dollars on supplies for my classroom. I bought books, pencils, paint, paper, construction paper, chalk, crayons, watercolors. If it was in my room, chances were high that I'd bought it. I even had to pay for my own photocopying. At both schools, teachers were discouraged from using the one copy machine in the office. The drugstore near my house had a copy machine, and it was open twenty-four hours. I often stopped there on my way to school to make last-minute copies. I would stand there, bathed in fluorescent light, shoving coins into the coin slot, making copies, and watching strange white women stumble out of the store carrying huge jugs of cheap vodka at 5:30 in the morning. When I moved to a different neighborhood, I spent so much time at Kinko's making copies that I developed a crush on one of the men who worked there.

Compton Unified School District did have a teacher re-source center. I visited it a few times. I liked going there because it had a nice bathroom with liquid soap rather than the pow-dered kind we had at our school. At an orientation for new teachers, we were told that we were allowed twenty-five pieces of construction paper each month. When we took the paper, though, we had to write down our name, our school, our grade level, and how many pieces of each color we were taking in a big three-ring binder. A woman was always sitting at the desk on which the binder was placed, seemingly guarding it. She never spoke to me, never even looked up when I recorded what I was taking in the book.

The resource center staff would laminate things for teach-ers, five feet worth every month. I loved having things lami-nated. I created large signs for my classroom: a giant test tube with purple bubbles to hang in the science area, a calendar for Amazing Equations, a fancy job wheel. I developed a strange obsession with all things laminated. I began to wonder if it would be possible to laminate things other than paper. I asked my roommate, also a teacher in Compton, if she thought it would be a good idea for me to laminate an outfit. Then I would just have to sponge off my clothes if they got dirty.

At the beginning of the school year at Garvey, every teacher was allowed to order one hundred dollars worth of supplies. Given that I had spent over three thousand dollars on supplies for my room the year before, one hundred dollars didn't seem like a lot, but it was something. All the teachers were sitting in the cafeteria during the first in-service day when Mrs. Carson, the principal, announced this good fortune. Immediately, one of the seasoned teachers yelled, "When are we going to get these supplies? February?"

I remember thinking, "Wow. She has a negative attitude. Maybe things were bad last year, but this year things will be different. She's not even giving it a chance." But this teacher knew what she was talking about. February came and went. Nothing ever arrived.

During that same first meeting at Garvey, we were told the district had purchased a new math curriculum. All the teachers were excited. However, when we were handed the materials for the new curriculum, we were given the teacher's edition of the workbook and a small white plastic box of supplies about the size of a shoebox. We were not given any student workbooks. Instead, we were told to white out the answers in the teacher's edition and Xerox the worksheets for our students. The teacher's edition suggested great lessons, but, in addition to not buying student workbooks, my school didn't buy all the materials necessary to implement the program. One lesson involved using color tiles to create patterns in order to illustrate the patterns found in multiplication tables. I looked in my small supply box. I had one set of tiles for the teacher to use on an overhead projector. I had no overhead, and there were no tiles for the students to use. The new math program, with all its good ideas, sat at the back of my room, collecting dust and mouse droppings.

Every year in Compton there were new promises. The district adopted a new math program, or hired a new superintendent, or initiated a new reading program, or bought a copy machine just for teachers. But the math program had no manipulatives, the superintendent left as quickly as he arrived, the reading program had no books, and the copy machine ran out of toner, which was never replaced. The hope that things would be different was what made teaching in Compton possible but also so hard. Without hope—mine and the students'— I wouldn't have lasted a week. I arrived full of hope, and I left defeated and disappointed, every single day.

Every month, at both schools where I worked, teachers were forced to participate in a kind of charade of hope. On the first day of the month we would find in our mailboxes a list of school supplies that were available: pencils, paper, folders, poster board, butcher paper, erasers, scissors, rulers. We could request those items we needed in our classrooms. Every month, I checked off the things I needed, usually most of the list. And then, sometimes, a week or two later, a student would arrive at my room carrying a brown box of supplies. I held my breath when I opened the box. Would I find what I needed inside? Usually there was a ream of paper, a box of ten pencils, and maybe a ruler or two. Sometimes no box ever arrived.

Hope got me out of bed in the morning, but it was anger that kept me from returning to bed when all I really wanted to do at the end of each day was crawl under the covers and scream. I was driven by spite and rage, which were effective, although not sustainable, motivators. I was also driven by my own ego. I had never failed at anything before in my life. I thought if I tried harder, loved my students more, bought more supplies, made more copies, got to school earlier, things would somehow be OK. I believed both that the shape of the schools in Compton was, somehow, my fault, and that I could be the one to help make it better. I lost fifteen pounds during my first three months as a teacher, and I dreamt the same nightmare almost every night. In my dream, I am in my classroom, but I cannot keep my eyes open. My students are climbing on desks, hanging on my waist. Sirens are wailing. Someone is hurt, and I am calling 9-1-1, but the operator will not help me. I start shouting and calling for help, but no one comes. And then I wake up.

In real life, people did come to help me. My students' parents, my own parents, my friends from college, my siblings, and other teachers offered support in the moments when I had begun to believe that I was all alone. I found myself longing for rescue and feeling guilty when it did, sometimes, come. More times than I wish to count, my privilege—in the form of plane tickets, vacations, credit cards, checks to help pay my rent— swooped in to carry me away. Such escapes soothed me for a short time, but I often felt emptier, more ashamed, more alone, when I returned. The people who gave me what I needed most were my students—these incredible children who showed up every day to learn, who devoured anything they could get their hands on, and who loved me with a fierce and protective love. Was their gift out of order? Was I wrong to keep taking it? Wasn't I the one there to give? The stories collected in this chapter reveal that where there should have been resources, there were none, and where I least expected to find them, there they were—resources that strengthened me and helped me through the day.

✎ ✎ ✎

Mr. Cleaver spent most days sitting at a low brown desk at the front of Madison Elementary School's supply room with his feet propped up on a chair watching television. His desk blocked the door. It was impossible to enter the storage room without climbing over his desk. I was never quite sure how he got behind his desk every morning. I never saw him climb over the desk. He was well over six feet tall and very skinny. I couldn't imagine him, dressed in a dark suit, hoisting one long leg and then the other over it, but I don't know how else he could have gotten into that room.

Mr. Cleaver was the keeper of supplies. In order to get lined writing paper, pencils, construction paper, poster board, chalk, paint, books, or anything else I might need, I had to ask him.

"Good morning, Mr. Cleaver," I would say.

"Good morning, Ms. Sentilles."

"Could I please have some pencils for my students?"

"Didn't I just give you some last month?"

"Yes, but you gave me one box of twelve. I have thirty-six students."

"Oh, that's too bad, but no, I don't think I have any more pencils."

Soon I started noticing other teachers bringing him food—

a box of doughnuts, a plate of cookies. I decided to give it a go. I bought a bag of Skittles at the grocery store and brought them to school.

"Good morning, Mr. Cleaver."

"Good morning, Ms. Sentilles."

I put the bag of Skittles on his desk. He looked down at the bag of candy and then back up at me.

"Could I please have some pencils for my students?" I asked.

"Why, of course. Please wait one minute while I get them for you." He disappeared into the back of the closet. He reappeared with several boxes of pencils, fat blue ones, the kind he knew my students liked but rarely gave me. These thick lead pencils were much better for learning how to write than the skinny yellow pencils that often broke under the pressure of a nervous six-year-old's fierce grip.

"Here you go," Mr. Cleaver said, loading my arms with boxes of pencils.

I figured candy was a strange but small price to pay for supplies. Skittles, Blow Pops, Tootsie Rolls. I brought candy; he gave me supplies. Not everything I needed, but more than the nothing he had given me before.

My experience at Madison with Mr. Cleaver was not an unusual one in Compton. A fourth grade teacher I knew at another elementary school in the district had a classroom that shared a wall with the supply closet; the back wall of her classroom was the back wall of the supply closet.

"Sarah," she said. "I think what is going to drive me crazy, what is going to push me over the edge, is the fact that all of the pencils and paper and notebooks I need are on the other side of my back wall. Three feet away. And no one will let me get to them." I suggested she try candy.

Every day after school I walked by Mr. Cleaver's office on my way to the parking lot. Every once in a while, his door would be open, but he would not be sitting at the desk. "Mr. Cleaver?" I would whisper, leaning over his desk to peer inside. If he was nowhere to be seen, I would climb over the desk, run inside, and grab as much of whatever supply I could find as quickly as I could. Then I would jump back over the desk, dragging my stolen goods behind me, and run to my car. I must have made a funny sight—running with my arms loaded with stacks of red construction paper or a box of cream-colored poster board or reams of writing paper. The trunk of my car became my own private supply closet, usually filled with stuff I didn't need.

When I first started teaching, I asked everyone for information about how I was supposed to teach my first grade students how to read. I was a literature major at Yale. I knew how to deconstruct texts. I had no idea how to help someone learn to read. Every teacher I asked suggested I use Rigby books. Rigby books came in both English and Spanish for grades 1 through 4. The easiest book might have one word per page, perhaps a picture of a beach ball and the word "ball." The hardest level had several paragraphs per page. The books came in sets of multiple copies of the same book, ideal for the Compton reading program, which required teachers to work with students in small groups during guided reading. I was dying to get my hands on these books. I started asking about them at the end of September. I wanted to know if we had any at Madison. The principal, Mrs. Redding, said no. Mr. Cleaver said no. My mentor teacher said no. My grade level chairperson said no. So I improvised. I went to the bookstore and bought Easy Readers, which approximate Rigby books. I bought one book per title and then took the books to Kinko's and made copies. Xeroxing is not an easy or cheap way to make books. During my first year as a teacher, I bought over fifty books. I Xeroxed each one of them, page by page, then I put the pages together and stapled them. I shared the books with other teachers. I think I kept my local Kinko's in business.

In March, we had a districtwide teacher in-service day about the Compton reading program for elementary school teachers. Every other word the facilitator said seemed to be "Rigby." You can use your Rigby books for this. You can use your Rigby books for that. Rigby books are perfect for this. Rigby books are perfect for that.

I had had enough. I raised my hand. The facilitator called on me. Before I spoke I looked around the room. Don't worry, folks, I hoped my glance would say. I'll let them know what it feels like to be told to use something that doesn't exist.

"Where would you suggest I find these Rigby books?" I asked in the most innocent tone I could muster. Just as I finished asking the question, Dr. Lawson, the head of the language arts program in Compton, walked through the door. The facilitator turned the question over to her.

"Rigby books were delivered to each school site in September," Dr. Lawson said.

"My school site doesn't have them."

"What is the name of your school?"

"Madison."

She looked down at the clipboard she was holding. "We delivered a complete set of Rigby books, English and Spanish, to your school in September."

September? I couldn't believe it. It was now March, seven months after the delivery, and no teacher at my school had been given any Rigby books. I drove straight to Madison after the inservice because I knew Mrs. Redding would still be working in her office. I saw her car in the parking lot. She stayed late every night. She stayed until 11:00 sometimes. She told me it made her husband nervous, but when it was time for her to die, it was time for her to die. And if it wasn't, she said, it was probably alright for her to stay late after school.

I parked my car and ran to her office. Mrs. Redding hadn't been the principal at Madison when the books were delivered at the beginning of the school year. She came at the end of September, replacing a previous principal who was promoted to a job at the district level.

I burst into her office. "We have Rigby books!" I shouted. "We have Rigby books!"

She got up from her desk. "I had no idea," she said. "They must be in Mr. Cleaver's office." We walked together to Mr. Cleaver's office. She unlocked the door. We climbed over the desk and began to look around. There, in the back corner of his office, were trays and trays of Rigby books, covered in a thin layer of dust.

We made several trips from his office to my classroom. We decided that I would be in charge of creating a checkout system for the books so all teachers could use them. We never mentioned to anybody that we stole the books from Mr. Cleaver's office.

Mr. Cleaver didn't mention it either.

✎ ✎ ✎

The second grade class at Garvey Elementary School went whale watching. Two classes of second graders—nearly seventy children and just two teachers—climbed onto a tiny boat and set sail. Most of my students had never been on a boat. When we left the dock, half of them were terrified and frozen in their seats, and the other half started to throw up. The students sat on benches lining the outside edge of the deck. A flimsy metal handrail separated them from the Pacific Ocean. We had no life jackets.

We had been traveling for over an hour, and we had not seen anything. No whales. No other boats. No fish. Nothing but a single seagull who followed our crowded boat. Dante Rogers, who sat next to me on the boat, turned to me and said, "Ms. Sentilles, this ain't no kind of whale watching. This is water watching."

In the beginning of second grade, Dante lived with his grandmother. During the first parent-teacher conference, ten weeks into the school year, I shared with Dante's grandmother how much I loved having him as a student. He laughed easily and worked hard, filling his papers with his tiny handwriting. At the end of the conference, Dante's grandmother told me Dante would be moving to a different school because he was moving back in with his mother. I was devastated. She told me Dante had been living with her temporarily because his mother had been addicted to drugs. His mother was finished with her rehab program, she said, and so Dante was going to live with her again.

"Oh," I said to his grandmother. "I wish he could stay with you."

When I said that, she looked at me and seemed to see through me, seeing the inexperienced kid I was. She said, "Honey, I'm glad he gets to live with his mom. I already raised my kids. I am proud of her, and he is excited to be with her again. He has missed her terribly."

Dante and his baby sister moved back in with their mother, but instead of moving him to another school closer to her house, she decided to let him stay in my class at Garvey. His mother was a frequent presence in my classroom. I saw her at the beginning of the day and at the end. She made sure Dante did all of his homework. She wrote long notes to me if she ever had any questions about what he was learning in school. And she packed him a huge lunch every single day.

Garvey provided a free breakfast and lunch for all children who qualified. To qualify, a family's income had to be below the poverty line. I think almost all of our students qualified, but when Dante moved back in with his mother, he started bringing his own food to school. He arrived each day with a snack for morning recess and a brown lunch bag filled with delicious food. Oranges divided into perfect triangles. Sandwiches cut in squares with no crusts. Bags of chips and cookies. While the rest of the class lined up to go to lunch or to recess, Dante would walk to the coat closet to dig through the chaotic pile of backpacks and coats until he found his blue backpack. He would unzip the backpack and take out his lunch or snack, and while he stood in line, he would unfold the piece of paper he found inside his lunch bag. His mother wrote him a note every day. I always tried to read over his shoulder: "Dear Dante, I just want you to know how proud I am of you. I love you, Mom" or "Dante, Have a great day. I miss you. Love, Mom" or "Dante, Do great in school. See you soon, baby. I love you, Mom." I think I looked forward to the notes more than Dante did. I needed them. Sometimes I would stand in the doorway of my classroom and watch him skip off to lunch or recess followed by several students who wanted some of whatever it was he had in his brown bag.

Ramon Rodriguez never brought his lunch to school. He was slight, with a head of long brown hair that often fell into his eyes. He spent much of the day flipping his head back to get the hair out of his eyes. He had the longest eyelashes I have ever seen on a human being. He never misbehaved in my room, but he liked to spend his time with the kids who did, an unusual combination. Ramon was extremely bright, he did everything he was ever asked to do in my classroom, and he did it well. His work was usually close to perfect. Most of the students in my classroom who did well did so because they liked to please me. Ramon did his work well because he could, not for me and not because he was supposed to. He always seemed to me quite detached from what was going on around him.

One morning during a lesson on language arts, Ramon walked over to the table where I was working with another group of students. "Ms. Sentilles, can I talk to you?" he asked. He was holding his stomach, and he looked like he was about to cry.

"Sure, Ramon." We walked together over to a corner of the classroom out of earshot of the other students. "What's going on?"

"My stomach hurts," he said.

"Do you think you have the flu?"

He shook his head. He pulled at my hand, bringing my head down to his level. "I'm really hungry," he said.

"Did you eat breakfast?" I asked.

"No." He put my hand on his stomach. He was so skinny his stomach felt concave. He started to cry, bending over in pain.

"Let's go get you some food," I said.

I told my class I would be right back, and I walked with Ramon, who was still clinging to my hand, across the yard and into the cafeteria. Almost all of our students qualified for Madison's free breakfast and lunch program. Without the free meals, many of my students would have spent the day at school hungry. Most of my students' parents worked several jobs to make ends meet, but still there never seemed to be enough money, food, or time.

Students could show up before school, between 7:00 and 7:30, for a hot breakfast. Ramon never came for the free breakfast. I had assumed he ate breakfast at home. I hoped there might be something left.

I walked into the cafeteria. A woman was mopping the floor.

"Excuse me," I said. "Do you think there might be any break-fast left for Ramon?"

She looked up from her work, and then she looked at Ramon. He was holding his stomach and my hand, trying to stand up straight, but bent because of the pain. "Of course," she said. "Come with me." We walked with her, and she prepared him a plate of waffles and syrup. She handed it to him and told him to go ahead and sit in the lunchroom. I walked him to a table. The room seemed strange, so silent and large with no students in it. Our footsteps echoed. He sat at one of the long tables, his feet dangling over the edge of the bench because they didn't yet reach the floor.

"Come back whenever you're done, Ramon," I said.

"I will, Ms. Sentilles," he said. "Thank you."

Most of my experiences in Compton were marked by scarcity —hungry children, missing textbooks, and ill-equipped class-rooms. One afternoon in December things were, briefly, differ-ent. Jamie Jones and I were sitting outside her classroom eating lunch when suddenly several huge white trucks and long black stretch limousines drove into the middle of the playground. Once they were parked, beautiful men in fancy suits began to pile out of the vehicles. Children at recess swarmed all around them.

"What's going on?" Jamie asked.

"I don't know," I said. "But I feel like I might be a bit too white for all this."

Soon the principal of Garvey, Mrs. Carson, appeared. She walked across the long stretch of asphalt between her office and the parked trucks and limousines. She greeted the visiting men. We watched from a distance as she shook each man's hand, nodding.

In a few minutes, we were directed to gather our students and bring them to the yard. "My students are eating lunch," I said.

"Well hurry them up," the assistant principal told me. "They won't want to miss this."

"Who are these people?" I asked.

"Death Row Records," she said. "They've come to give every student a Christmas gift."

I did as I was told. I gathered my students from the cafeteria and lined them up with hundreds of other students. We must have waited for over forty-five minutes. When we got to one of the trucks, each student was handed a new, still packaged toy —huge water guns, toy trucks, big sets of Matchbox cars, dolls. The students were elated. Every teacher was given a Christmas record album and a poster publicizing the album. The cover was a picture of a black Santa Claus, strapped to an electric chair, with a hood over his head.

I knew all about Death Row Records. I loved hip-hop and rap. Suge Knight, the CEO of Death Row Records, grew up in Compton and played professional football for the Los Angeles Rams. He retired from football in 1990, became a bodyguard for Bobby Brown, and two years later formed Death Row Records. Dr. Dre, Snoop, and Tupac Shakur, some of the biggest names in rap music, were produced by Death Row Records, one of the most successful labels in rap and hip-hop in the 1990s. At the time Death Row Records visited Garvey, Knight was in jail. While in prison, according to the company website, Knight made sure that Death Row Records continued the outreach programs he had created: handing out free Thanksgiving turkeys to the homeless, providing free transportation on Father's Day for children whose fathers are incarcerated, supplying legal funds for those who can't afford representation, and hosting an annual Mother's Day party for single moms.

After all the toys had been delivered, teachers stood and talked with the men from Death Row Records, posing for pictures, laughing, and asking Baby Face, one of the label's newest stars, to sing. Then, as quickly as they had come, they were gone.

"Why toys?" I kept thinking to myself after the overfilled trucks had disappeared. I even asked the question out loud to Mrs. Carson. "Why toys?" I asked her.

"It's Christmas," she said, looking at me like I was out of my mind.

But we need so much here, I wanted to answer, but didn't.

The generosity of Compton families often overwhelmed me. With so little, they shared so much.

Eleana Dominguez, one of my second grade students at Garvey Elementary, read at an eighth grade level in English. She was the best reader in my classroom. Both her parents spoke and read Spanish. When I asked who had taught her to read English so well, Eleana shook her head, shrugged her shoulders, and said, "I don't know. Me, I guess."

Eleana arrived at school every day wearing a spotless dress with matching shoes. Her long, dark hair was braided and fastened with colorful barrettes or ribbons. She brought her homework every day, perfect answers written in perfect handwriting. She never missed a single day of school.

Eleana had a younger sister and a younger brother. Every day after school, her mother and her two siblings waited for her at the gate. Her brother and sister were always so excited to see Eleana that they would break through the group of parents lined at the gate and run toward her the minute they saw her walk out of our classroom.

One Saturday afternoon, I took Eleana to the Los Angeles County Museum of Art. When I brought her home, Mrs. Dominguez was waiting at the gate at the end of their driveway. She invited me to come inside her home.

She led me past clotheslines covered in socks and sheets and little girls' dresses, past an enormous orange tree, past a wall covered in graffiti, to the front door of her family's apartment. The Dominguez family—all five of them—lived in the garage at the end of the driveway. The garage had been converted into a duplex, and they lived in one half of this. Their entire apartment—one bedroom and a kitchen—could have fit in the living room of my own apartment. The tiny kitchen was crammed with a small round table, four chairs, a highchair, and a refrigerator covered in brightly colored magnets. There was no way to walk around the table without climbing over chairs. A doorway led from the kitchen to a bedroom the size of a walk-in closet. In the room were a set of bunk beds, a crib, and a dresser.

Mrs. Dominguez invited me to sit at the kitchen table. She offered me a Coca-Cola. To make room for me, she had to move a typewriter that was taking up half the table. In Spanish, I asked Mrs. Dominguez whose typewriter it was.

"It's mine," Eleana answered in English.

"What do you do with it, Eleana?"

"I type things."

"Like what?"

"Stories."

Mrs. Dominguez handed me a Coke, and we sat at the table and drank together. I pointed at the magnets covering the refrigerator and said, "Que bonitas." Immediately, Mrs. Dominguez stood and told Eleana to pick a magnet for me to take home.

I looked around the apartment and wondered where Eleana found space to do her homework. "Where do you do your schoolwork, Eleana?" I asked.

She sipped her Coke, her hand too small to fit all the way around the can, and pointed to the bedroom. "In there," she said.

"Where in there?" I asked.

"On the bottom bed."

Where Eleana actually did her homework and where I had imagined Eleana did her homework were dramatically different. In my mind, she had a desk, a lamp, a chair—a quiet space all her own. In reality, she had the soft surface of a bottom bunk in a room she shared with her entire family.

"What do you do when you finish your homework?" I asked.

"I type stories or I play school with my sister."

"Are you the teacher or the student?"

"I like to be the teacher," she said.

When it was time for me to leave, Mrs. Dominguez and Eleana walked with me to the end of the driveway. They stopped at the orange tree and filled two grocery bags with oranges for me to take home. I left with my hands full—two bags of oranges, a cold Coke for my roommate, and a magnet.

"My mom says please visit any time," Eleana told me as I climbed into my car.

✎ ✎ ✎

Every morning Kendol Law walked his brother Wendol from their mother's car to Wendol's kindergarten classroom. The separation was new to him each day, as if he were saying goodbye to his brother for the first time. I would watch Kendol put his small arm around Wendol's shoulders, comforting him. And then he would return to our line, crying. He cried every single morning. He would cling to my arm, hugging me. "What happened, Kendol?" I would ask, as if I hadn't asked the same question the morning before.

"I took Wendol to kindergarten."

"Kendol, you take Wendol to kindergarten every day."

"I know. I just miss him," he would cry.

"It's OK to miss him, Kendol, but it's important for you both to go to school. Wendol likes kindergarten."

"I know, Ms. Sentilles. I just wish we could be together forever."

Kendol looked like a collection of bones and tendons. The best word to describe him is "taut." His skin seemed stretched too tight, pulled almost to the breaking point. He was the most emotional seven-year-old I had ever met. He sobbed, he cried so hard he couldn't breathe, he collapsed on the floor, he pretended to faint, and occasionally he laughed so hard he fell out of his chair. He played on a basketball team. He had red glasses he refused to wear. Sometimes he wore a small gold hoop in one ear, when he wanted to look like a pirate.

Kendol loved everyone as much as he loved his brother, and he showed his love dramatically. He was keenly aware of what was going on with everyone in the classroom, and without fail, he befriended whoever was being excluded: the new student, a student who didn't speak any English, the one white student who was dirty and covered in lice, the student who couldn't sit still for more than sixty seconds. He took each of them under his wing, making sure they had someone to sit with at lunch or to play with at recess. As the class lined up to go to recess or lunch, Kendol would come up to me and ask if he could whisper something in my ear.

"Ms. Sentilles," he would whisper, "I think Elise looks sad, don't you?"

"I do, Kendol."

"Well, you know what I'm gonna do? I'm gonna be her best friend."

"That's very nice, Kendol," I would say. Then I would watch him walk to the line and stand next to Elise or whomever he had decided needed extra attention that day.

One day Kendol was on his way to the bathroom when he

saw an ambulance parked outside another second grade classroom. A second grade student was having a seizure. Kendol looked inside the room to see what was happening and witnessed everything: the writhing, the screaming, the medical technicians tying the girl to a portable bed, the IV, the shots to calm her down.

Ms. Ballard, the teacher of the student who was having the seizure, saw Kendol at the back of the room. And then she saw him run out of her classroom. She couldn't find him, and so she came to find me, to tell me what Kendol had seen.

I went to look for Kendol on the yard. When I found him, he was standing with a group of friends, laughing.

"Hi, Kendol," I said.

"Hey, Ms. Sentilles."

"I heard you might have seen something upsetting."

"I did, Ms. Sentilles," he said, and he began to cry hysterically.

"Did you know her name, Kendol?"

"No. But I saw her. She was very sick and was yelling and had to go to the hospital."

"She's OK now, Kendol. They are going to take good care of her in the hospital."

"You know why I am crying so much, Ms. Sentilles?"

"No, Kendol. Why?"

"Because she was my best friend."

"You didn't even know her name, Kendol."

"I know I didn't. But I think she's my best friend."

Kendol had the largest vocabulary of any second grader in my class. The words he chose and the phrases he put together were very grown up. What was odd was that while he spoke like an adult, his handwriting looked like that of a three-year-old. He never did his schoolwork. I think the entire time I was his teacher he finished three assignments. His mother and I met often to talk about his refusal to do his work, but nothing we tried seemed to help.

Every other teacher at Garvey loved Kendol. He made them laugh, gave them hugs, told them jokes and stories, took care of their students. He was an amazing and delightful person outside the classroom; inside the classroom—during academic time—he was extremely difficult. He refused to participate in language arts centers. Sometimes he would curl up in a corner and stay there for the entire day. He didn't care if I took away his recess, if I called his mother, if I sent him to another classroom, if he went late to lunch, if I took away his painting privileges. I completed the paperwork to have him referred to the special education program, but by the end of the year, it had still not been processed.

I started not to bother with Kendol in the classroom. I ignored his emotional outbursts. I ignored his messy desk. I ignored the fact that he refused to do his work. I had thirty-five other students. I couldn't stop to figure out what was wrong with Kendol every time he started to cry. He cried several times a day.

When his mother came to the final parent-teacher conference at school, Kendol showed her his desk. The desks in my classroom were arranged in groups of six or eight so the students could participate in group work. Kendol's desk was not in one of these groups. His desk was at the front of the classroom, the only single desk in the room. It was pushed up against the chalkboard. He had asked me if he could sit by himself. He could concentrate better, he said. I liked having him at the front of the room because I could put my hand on his shoulder while I was teaching to make sure he was paying attention. His mother looked at his desk, alone at the front of the room. Then she pulled the trash can over and started to empty his desk. The inside compartment of Kendol's desk was packed with trash, old papers, toys, crumpled and incomplete schoolwork. She even found an old McDonald's hamburger. I watched as his mother cleaned his desk. I felt my face get hot. I was embarrassed that she was cleaning his desk. I was ashamed that I hadn't noticed how filthy it was. I was angry with myself for not collecting his schoolwork. What must she be thinking?

Kendol participated in Garvey Elementary School's after-school tutoring program. The program was a last-ditch effort to help prepare students to take the California Achievement Test (CAT-5). I was one of the second grade tutors. With Trena Ballard, the teacher whose second grader had had the seizure, I taught more than thirty second graders on Tuesday and Thursday afternoons. Although the tutoring program was supposed to help students who were not succeeding in a regular classroom setting, because there were so many students who needed extra attention, it merely re-created that setting.

Part of the program, known as "Write to Learn," involved working in the upper grades' computer lab. The second grade was the only grade level that didn't have access to the computer lab during the regular school day. The second grade's lab was being used as a classroom, the computers unplugged and pushed against the wall to make room for students and desks. The second grade students in the tutoring program were excited to have a chance to use the computers.

I took a group of eleven students, one of them Kendol, to the Write to Learn lab. The students sat in front of the computers and followed the computer teacher's instructions. They were told to type their names, to find the space bar, to type the alphabet. Most students seemed to have no problem following these instructions. I looked over at Kendol. He was sitting still, staring at the computer screen.

"What's going on, Kendol?" I asked.

"I can't find the letters in my name," he said.

I looked at the keyboard of his computer. The letters s, k, l, and n were rubbed off. He couldn't type "Kendol Law" because some of the letters in his name were no longer on the keyboard. The words "Shift" and "Delete" were also missing. The computer immediately next to Kendol's was marked "Out of Order," so I asked the computer teacher if I could switch Kendol's keyboard with the intact keyboard belonging to the broken computer.

"No, you can't do that," she said.

"Why?" I asked.

"Because this equipment doesn't belong to you. It belongs to the district."

"But Kendol can't learn to type on a keyboard that's missing letters and keys."

"Yes, he can. Everyone else has learned to use that computer. He just has to compensate."

I had another suggestion. "If I can't switch the keyboards, can I at least use a black marker to write the missing letters on the keys?"

"No. Absolutely not. These computers are not yours to mess with. They belong to the district."

I looked around the room. There were about twenty computers. Only twelve of them were functioning. The rest had missing parts or letters like Kendol's or were marked "Out of Order." I turned my attention back to Kendol. I put my hands on his shoulders. "OK, Kendol, we're just going to have to try to do the best we can with what we have."

The second grade at Garvey Elementary School took a field trip to the Forrest Lawn Cemetery to visit the museum there. As we drove through the cemetery, Denver Carraway began to cry. A few days earlier, her uncle had been shot and killed in his driveway. He was washing his car when a stray bullet hit him in the head and killed him. Denver missed one day of school for the funeral. When Kendol saw Denver crying, he immediately burst into tears. The sight of the graves and tombstones and Denver's tears was too much for him. He crawled through the aisle of the bus, found me, and collapsed in my lap. I rocked him in my arms and let him weep.

I began to believe Kendol carried inside him all the woundedness of Compton. It was Kendol who reacted for all of us. He wept for the collapsing ceilings. He cried about the rusted metal bars on the playground. He sobbed for the missing textbooks, the maggots crawling on our floors, the ignored special education referrals. He screamed for the gunshots and the dying and the broken. Kendol refused to participate in the daily routine of being a student. He said "no" while the rest of us tried to pretend that everything was fine, that the school was normal, that it was OK for it to be raining inside a classroom because it rained outside, that a condemned building covered in graffiti was adequate. While we tried to make the best of it, to ignore everything, to put all of those images in another place far away from our daily reality, Kendol felt, absorbed, witnessed. He made our hidden wounds his own. Our alienation, our anger, our profound sadness—he felt them, and he wept for us all.

During the first month that I was a teacher at Garvey, I lost my ability to see. My second graders were working on math problems at their desks. I was circulating around the room helping individual students who needed me. I had to bend down to work with them. I started having trouble seeing their papers. I thought at first it was simply because all the blood was rushing to my head from bending up and down. But it didn't pass. I couldn't see my students' work, and then I couldn't see my students. I asked everyone to remain in their seats, and I opened my classroom door, hoping someone would be outside who could help me. We didn't have an intercom system, so I had no way of contacting the office. I sent one student to the office to get help. I sat down to wait. Kendol sat next to me.

"What's wrong, Ms. Sentilles?" he asked.

"I can't see, Kendol."

Kendol took my hand in his tiny one and said, "Don't worry. You're going to be OK. You will be able to see real soon. Everything is going to be all right. I'm right here."

The principal drove me to the closest emergency room, and

I was, eventually, able to see again. I sat on a cold metal table, and the emergency room doctor told me I either had a brain tumor or a migraine. I told him he had no bedside manner. Tests eventually showed that the blindness was a symptom of a migraine, but I knew that during my time of lost vision something had shifted. I saw differently. I saw myself differently. I saw my students differently. As seven-year-old Kendol held my hand and soothed me, I knew I belonged in my classroom. But I also knew I couldn't stay.

CHAPTER V
A KIND OF BELONGING

AMY LEVINSON, a sixth grade teacher in Compton and my roommate during my first year in Los Angeles, came home one day after school laughing. "You will never guess what happened today, Sarah," she said.

"What?" I asked. We didn't have a couch yet, so I was sitting in a butterfly chair, my legs over the edge, eating soup and watching television. I muted the volume.

"Two of my students, Deon and Rickie, were hanging out in my room after school while I was grading papers, and Deon was saying a whole bunch of stuff about Caucasians. He was going off saying, 'Caucasians this' and 'Caucasians that.' The whole time Rickie was looking at him, gesturing madly toward me. Deon finally noticed and stopped. 'What?' he asked. Then Rickie said, 'Deon, I think Ms. Levinson is white.' Deon stood there, stunned. He looked at me, then turned back to Rickie. 'Man,' he said, 'she's not white.' 'Oh, really,' I said. 'What am I, then?' He paused and then he looked at me and said, 'You're black.'"

Amy is a white Jewish woman, with pale skin and dark brown hair. Deon's words revealed an understanding of race based not just on skin color but on behavior. Amy didn't behave how white people behaved in Deon's experience, so she wasn't white. She belonged.

I, too, found a kind of belonging in Compton that I never expected to find. I wore my keys and a whistle around my neck at school and wherever I went in Compton. These objects hanging around my neck marked me as a teacher, and because I was a teacher, people in the community regarded me, if not as an insider, then at least as a person with an established role in the community. No matter where I went in Compton—the gas station, the grocery store, a fast food place for lunch—people greeted me with a question about school.

I belonged—and at the same time, I didn't belong. I had been sent to Compton, not invited. I was dropped into that community, a colonialist, a missionary believing I carried something Compton needed, when so many had come before me. And still, people in the community embraced me, especially my students. Every morning, I would pull into the school's driveway, drive through the gate, and see six or seven students waiting in my usual parking space for me. Once I had parked, they surrounded my car, tapping on the glass of my windows, calling my name, before I even opened the door.

One day after school, near Mother's Day, Eliot Carleton and his mother came to visit me in my classroom. Eliot carried a large pink envelope in his hand.

"Hi, Ms. Sentilles," he said. "We have something for you." He handed me the envelope.

"Can I open it now?" I asked.

"Of course," his mother said.

I opened the card. It was about as big as a notebook, covered with pink and red roses. These words were written on the card in beautiful cursive writing: "Happy Mother's Day. You are like a mother to me."

Many of the people I met in Compton made gestures like Eliot's to include me. I was invited to homes for dinner, to sons' football games, to the mall to shop for a new outfit for African Heritage Day, to go dancing with other young faculty members. Mothers brought me homemade tamales. Parents confided in me. Younger brothers and sisters of my students brought me drawings they had made. I was given oranges and rings and necklaces. There were also countless ways in which it was made clear to me that I didn't belong. Meetings about which I was never told. Parties to which I was not invited. A faculty lounge that fell silent when I walked in. Whispers, laughter, rolled eyes. I was surrounded by people, but I often felt alone. What was my relationship with the children and families I met in Compton? Sometimes I felt like an adopted daughter, other times like a mother, other times like an uninvited visitor everyone wanted to go away.

By the end of my first year in Compton, Deon, the student who thought my white friend Amy was black, was dead. No foster home could be found for him, and so he had been sent to a home for boys. Another boy at the home beat him to death with a brick. I remember the day Amy told me about Deon's murder, but I can't remember if we even cried.

I have cried often since. There is not a day that goes by, walking on the brick-lined streets of my new neighborhood, that I don't think of Deon, a student I met only once. What am I to make of these haunting images that return to me, both when

I am awake and when I sleep? This chapter is full of such images—burning houses, dead mothers, and flashing knives. It is
also full of images of incredible beauty and strength—laughter, mothers, and bubbles. What kind of relationship do these
images forge between me and Compton, between me and these
children, dead and alive? What was a radicalizing and life-
changing experience for me was just two years in their regular
lives. And yet their images, the ones I have turned into words
in this book, form, for me, a family album of sorts. These are the
stories of the people I hold myself accountable to, people who
have shaped who I am and who I want to be, people who remind me where I belong. I carry these images with me. They
weigh on me like precious stones.

On the first day of school at Garvey Elementary School, while
I was holding a sign that said, "Ms. Sentilles, Room 18, Second
Grade," Loretta Mavely ran up to me, dragging her mother behind her, and said, "Look, Mama, look! My teacher looks just
like me." When I looked at Loretta, I felt like I was looking
in a mirror. She was the only white student I ever taught in
Compton.

When I was in Houston at the Teach for America Summer
Institute, I attended a workshop run by a woman who spoke
about teachers who had personality clashes with their students.
"Sometimes," the woman said, "you will find you just don't like
a certain student. And let me tell you, it's hard to teach a stu-

dent you don't like." Surely that will not happen to me, I remember thinking.

Then I met Loretta. It was hard for me to teach Loretta. I didn't like her. At all. But there was no particular reason I didn't like her. She was very smart. She was an excellent artist. She was great at math. She usually did her homework.

But she was filthy dirty. Visibly dirty. Her arms were streaked with dirt. Her hair was crawling with lice—white and brown flakes I could see moving when I leaned down to help her at her desk. Her clothes were stained and wrinkled. Her homework was sometimes wet, muddy, or covered in fruit punch. Even her food stamps—which she periodically brought out of her pocket to show me—were crinkled and dirty.

Students were cruel to Loretta. If she touched something— a classroom ball, a jump rope, a pencil—they would refuse to touch it after she had. They taunted her. They refused to play with her at recess. They made fun of her mother. They told her to take a bath. She would come to me, crying, almost every day after recess.

"What's wrong, Loretta?" I would ask.

"No one will be my friend," she would say.

"What's going on?"

"They're teasing me."

"What are they saying?"

"They told me to go get me some soap and take a bath 'cause I'm dirty."

I would then find the students who had been bothering her and take away their recess, write notes home, or call their parents. I knew how to punish those students, how to change their behavior, but I didn't know how to make Loretta feel better. I was sure their words were wounding her, but I didn't know what to say. They were right. She did need to take a bath.

I didn't behave much better than the students who bothered Loretta. Loretta loved to hold my hand. I had to force myself to hold her hand. Throughout the day, she would run up to me and throw her arms around me and give me a big hug. I was sure I was going to get lice.

I decided to talk to the principal, Mrs. Carson, about Loretta. Maybe together we could find a way to help Loretta and her family. "Ms. Sentilles," Mrs. Carson said, "we have been dealing with Loretta's mother for years now. Her kids always come to school dirty."

"What should I do?"

"There's nothing to do."

"But no one is taking care of her, and she has so many lice I can see them crawling all over her head."

"Ms. Sentilles," Mrs. Carson said, "I visited her house, and let me tell you, to get rid of the lice in that house, we'd have to burn the whole thing down."

Periodically Loretta would come to school with a short new haircut. The back of her head would be shaved, or she would have bangs cut almost to her hairline. I think those haircuts —which made it look like a small child had taken scissors to her hair—were her mother's attempts to get rid of the lice. Or maybe they were Loretta's attempts. I imagined her cutting her own hair: sitting on the floor, gripping a pair of scissors, surrounded by blond hair, and cutting. Cutting. Cutting.

Loretta had two siblings at Garvey, a sister named Letty in the fourth grade and a brother named Michael in the fifth grade. Michael was rarely in class. He wandered around the campus all day long. His teacher, sick of trying to convince him to stay in the room, gave up and let him wander. He was a huge boy, tall and wide with bright red hair and freckles. When I saw the three Mavely children walking together—to or from school—I could hear Michael yelling at Loretta. He would swear at her and tell her to shut up. Sometimes when he was wandering around the school, he yelled her name in a high-pitched frightening voice, "Looorr-eeeeeeeeee-taaaa. Oh, Looorr-eeeeeeeeee-taaaa."

In the middle of the year, Loretta started spending her recess time with two girls from my class, Eva and Sandra. They were constantly late for everything. Late coming in from recess. Late to school in the morning. Late finishing their schoolwork. One day, I planned to do a painting project immediately after lunch recess. We were going to make a series of watercolor paintings based on the artwork of Joan Miró. Before I took my class to lunch, I reminded everyone we didn't have much time for the project, so it was important to be in line on time after recess. If they were late, I told them, they wouldn't be allowed to paint.

After recess, I went to meet my class. My students, except Loretta, Eva, and Sandra, were standing in two perfect lines waiting for me. They were clearly excited to paint.

"Where are Loretta, Eva, and Sandra?" I asked.

"In the bathroom playing with water and bothering people," my class said, practically in unison.

I had sent note after note home to their parents about the three girls being late to class. The campus is not safe, I wrote to their families, and it is not a good idea for your children to wander around by themselves. "OK," I said to my class, "let's hurry up and get inside before they see us. I guess they won't get to do the project."

All of a sudden I was acting like a second grader. I was running away from my own students. My entire class, with me at the front of the line, started running toward our room. I opened the door and let them slide, one by one, under my arm. Usually I had all the students shake my hand before they came into the room. This time I just said, "Hurry up, hurry up, hurry up." As the last student came into the classroom, I saw the three girls running across the campus to try to make it into the room before I closed the door. They were waving at me and shouting, "Wait! Wait for us!" I turned around and slammed the classroom door.

When they knocked on the door, I didn't answer. The students in my room were silent, watching to see what I was going to do next. The three girls knocked again, and this time I let them in. "You're late," I said. "Go stand by my desk."

They stood and watched as I passed out the painting supplies to the rest of the class. Then one of my students said, "Ooooohhh, Ms. Sentilles, Loretta's making faces at you."

I turned around and looked at the three girls. Sandra was standing quietly. Eva was standing quietly. Loretta was standing, glaring at me, pursing her lips, and rocking her head back and forth, back and forth. "Loretta," I said, "you can just take your attitude and put it in the trash can because that's where it belongs." I then let Eva and Sandra start painting while I left Loretta, alone, standing at my desk.

• • •

Sometimes I imagined Loretta's life: she woke up in a house filled with filth and stale food and lice; she walked to school with a brother who yelled at her; she went to an unsafe school where kids teased her and refused to touch her, and the teacher, who looked just like her, didn't protect her; and then she returned home to the same dirty house to see her mother, who wore fishnet stockings to parent-teacher conferences and was rumored to be a prostitute.

I don't know exactly why I actively disliked Loretta. I think, maybe, it was because she did look so much like me. I looked at her blond hair, her blue eyes, her freckled face, and I saw myself as a seven-year-old. The similarities made the differences more obvious. Looking at Loretta, I saw the thin line between where I was and where she would be. Looking at Loretta, how could I be proud of myself for graduating from Yale? How was that my achievement? Was I smarter than Loretta? No. My family just had more money than hers. The communities we called home were based on nothing other than circumstances of birth. The same was true of all the students in my class. Privilege, not merit, separated us.

I created distance between me and Loretta. I blamed her for her dirty clothes, for her lice, for her muddy skin, as if she were in control of when she got to take a bath or when her clothes were washed or when her hair was shampooed. As if there were something clearly wrong with her. I blamed Loretta, and then I blamed her mother. But Loretta probably spent more time with me than she spent with her mother, probably spent more time at school, in my classroom, than in her own home. But instead of giving her some sign that maybe she was worth something, the school showed her more of what she had already seen. She had a dirty house, and she attended a dirty school. She had a head full of lice, and she studied in a classroom with maggots crawling on the floor. She had a brother who yelled at her, and she had a teacher who did more of the same.

✎ ✎ ✎

Simone Roberts's mother committed suicide when Simone was in first grade. Simone and her sister, Danielle, found their mother hanging in the bathroom of their home. Simone was in my second grade class at Garvey Elementary School. She couldn't read. She couldn't write. She couldn't sit still. She shouted. She hit her desk. She raged in my classroom.

Immediately after their mother died, Simone and Danielle lived with Loretta's family in their dirty, lice-ridden house. At some point, they moved in with their grandmother, a woman I sometimes saw after school when she pulled up in a long Cadillac to pick up her granddaughters.

Simone had a smile that lit up her entire face. She was a beautiful girl, tall and striking. She had the most unusual belly button I have ever seen; it was as big as a cork. I saw her belly button—although I tried to avoid staring at it—because she always lost a few buttons on her white school uniform shirt during the day. When she stretched, her belly button would pop out between the missing buttons.

Simone didn't sit in her seat like other students. I would look at her while I was teaching a lesson and she would be sitting backward, her head leaning against the desk and her feet thrown over the back of her chair. Sometimes one arm would be on the ground. Other times both arms would be inside her desk. She would always be talking to herself or to her neighbor.

"Simone Roberts," I would say.

"Whu?" she would answer. Simone never said "what." She always said "whu" and looked at me as if she had no idea why I might be singling her out.

"Why do you think I said your name?" I would ask.

"Oh, yeah," she would say as she readjusted her seating position. "Sorry, Ms. Sentilles."

This became a ritual. Three or four times a day I had to stop and say her name because she was flailing around in her chair. At least once a day she fell out of her seat. So many students fell out of their seats that we started keeping a classroom tally on the chalkboard. Our goal was to try to keep it under three students a day. I always thought it was funny that I had a job that involved people spontaneously falling out of chairs.

I got tired of interrupting lessons to remind Simone how to sit. And I got tired of her saying "whu?" as if she had no idea why I was annoyed. So I made a rule.

"Simone?"

"Whu?" I just looked at her. "Oh, yeah. Sorry, Ms. Sentilles."

"I'm making a new rule just for you. If you say 'whu' when I say your name, you automatically have to go late to lunch."

"OK. I'll try to remember that, Ms. Sentilles."

In December, the three students from the lowest reading group, Simone's reading group, were still in the lowest reading group, and we were still working on beginning sounds, struggling to read books with one or two words on each page. I was frustrated with myself and with my students. I didn't know if I was doing something wrong. Maybe they knew they were in the lowest group and that affected their confidence. Maybe what was going on in their homes was affecting their ability to read. I didn't know what else to try, what other tricks to use, who to ask for help. During one reading period, these three students sensed my growing frustration, got nervous, and started to guess words, not even attempting to read them. I got mad. "Look," I said in an annoyed voice. "All I want you to do is at least say a word that starts with the same letter as the word on the page. If the book says 'car' and you read the word as 'cat' or 'cut' or 'can' or anything else that starts with a *c* that's OK, but if you say 'mat' or 'sad' or 'tree' I am going to be very upset."

Threatening students is definitely not a good way to teach them how to read. They looked at me. They looked anxious.

It was Simone's turn to read. The word was "whale." Simone just sat and looked at me.

"Don't look at me, Simone. Look at the word."

She stared hard at the open book.

"OK, Simone," I said. "What is the first sound in that word?"

Simone said the name of the first letter, "w."

"Yes, that is the name of the first letter. What sound does that letter make?"

She looked at me, looked at the word, looked back at me, and then made the strangest sound I have ever heard. She sounded like a squawking bird inhaling deeply and choking on a stick.

"Simone, the word is 'whale,'" I said. I closed my book, and then I reached across the table and closed all their books, too. I called the next group to come read with me.

Because of her mother's death, Simone had not attended first grade for most of the year. I didn't find out that she had missed almost an entire year of school until the end of her second grade school year. No one—not her grandmother, not her first grade teacher, not the principal—told me she had missed first grade, and it never occurred to me to ask. It never occurred to me that maybe this was the reason she didn't know her letters or her numbers or how to sit in her seat or how to pay attention. Simone missed this crucial year, and instead of retaining her in first grade, Garvey Elementary School passed her to the next grade. Compton Unified School District discouraged retention and used a policy informally called "social promotion." The district lost money for students who were retained. Even when parents and teachers asked for students to be retained, the district passed them to the next grade. As a result, some students made it all the way to sixth grade not knowing how to read.

Simone and I fought with each other every day—about how she sat in her seat, about using an inside voice, about paying attention, about writing her letters the same size. But we also loved each other. Every morning, as I was walking from my car to my classroom, Simone would see me from across the campus and come running at me, as fast as she could, arms spread wide like she was flying. When she reached me, she would fling her arms around my waist and say, "I am so happy to see you. I missed you. Good morning."

When she was absent, she left an empty space in the classroom larger than the absence of other students. With Simone in the room, things were never still or quiet. She was constantly moving or talking or having a temper tantrum. When she was not in school, the room was calmer, revealing how her frantic energy dominated the classroom. But I missed her morning hugs. I missed her huge smile.

When I walked my class to the gate to meet their families after school, Simone would hug me before she ran off in the direction of the office to meet her sister, Danielle. One day as she hugged me she said, "Ms. Sentilles, I wish you were my mom."

"I would be lucky to have a daughter like you, Simone."

"I wish you could be my mom and I could ride in your car and come home with you and see your cat and live with you forever."

"I think the rest of your family would miss you, Simone," I said.

"I miss my mom, Ms. Sentilles," Simone said. She stood next to me, still, one of the only times I remember her standing that way. I reached out for her hand. I felt like I was home. I heard Danielle calling her name. Simone hugged me and ran off, arms flying, backpack bouncing, laughing as she shouted, "I'm coming, Danielle! Bye, Ms. Sentilles! See you tomorrow."

✎ ✎ ✎

I looked forward to seeing Andre Asher every day. His mind, sense of humor, and legs were equally quick. At age seven, Andre had the personality of someone three times his age. Often I forgot he was seven. Then he would cry because he had lost a dollar on the playground, and I would remember.

During a lesson I was teaching on emotions at Garvey, students had to come to the front of the classroom, choose an index card out of a hat, and act out the emotion written on the card. Andre was one of the first students chosen to act because the other students loved his acting so much. When it was his turn, Andre whispered in my ear that he wanted to choose his own emotion instead of using one of the emotions from the hat. He began to act. He limped across the room, from one side of the rug to the other, right arm swinging in front of his body, left arm hanging still behind his back. "Hey, man," he said, "check out my new Nikes. Hey, I'm cool. Yeah, that's right." The emotion: pride.

Andre was very good at math. Every morning as part of our morning routine, we generated as many "Amazing Equations" as we could for the date. If it was October 27, for example, students created as many equations as they could for the number 27. I used Amazing Equations to teach my students higher-level mathematics. If one student said, "$20 + 7 = 27$," another student would say, "Flip it," and we would change the equation to "$7 + 20 = 27$." Through "flip it," my second grade students learned the associative property of addition. They also learned to flip the equation in a different way: $20 + 7 = 27$ could be turned around to read $27 - 7 = 20$. Flipping the equations in this way, my students discovered that addition and subtraction were inverse operations.

When we learned multiplication, Andre made the mental

leap that multiplication and division were inverse operations. I was standing outside on the black asphalt surveying the regular morning scene: mothers with strollers, a sandy stray dog chasing a group of screaming children, fifteen students hanging on the rusty jungle gym, a long line of students waiting to get into the cafeteria for the free hot breakfast. Looking at the chaos, I felt tired. I could feel the sun beating down on me; it was hot at only 7:45 in the morning. I was exhausted. I wasn't sure I could make it through the day. Then Andre ran up to me, wrapped his arms around me, and said in an excited voice, "Hey, Ms. Sentilles, I can divide! It's just like with addition and subtraction. All you have to do is flip the multiplication equation. See? Come on, ask me one." And all at once I remembered why I came to school.

"OK, Andre," I said, "What is 14 divided by 7?"

"2. That's easy. Give me a harder one."

"64 divided by 8?"

"8."

"121 divided by 11?"

"11," he said quickly, a proud grin spreading across his face. He took my hand, and we walked to the line where the rest of our class was waiting.

Andre's mother, Mona Asher, paid him one dollar for each A he received on his report card. Because he usually received all As from me, he made quite a bit of money off his report card. During parent-teacher conferences after the first quarter, Mona laughed and said, "I'm going to have to get another job to pay for this boy's report card." At the end of the second quarter, I passed out the report cards in sealed envelopes. The students were supposed to take the envelopes home and open them with their parents. When I gave Andre his envelope, he immediately held it out in front of him and said, "Please, Jesus. Anything that is not an A, please change it. Come on, Jesus."

Before Father's Day, we wrote poems to celebrate fathers. Before writing, though, we brainstormed a list of things that a "father" does: loves us, goes to work, brings home money for food, takes us to the park, takes us fishing, walks us to school. I then explained that on Father's Day, it was OK to give a present or a card or a hug to whoever did these things for them. The person, I explained, might be an uncle, a mother, an older brother, or a grandmother. For our Father's Day present, we wrote poems describing ourselves using metaphors. When the poems were finished, we mounted each poem on a big piece of construction paper and painted a border around it.

While my students worked on their poems, I walked around the room helping them spell words. When I arrived at Andre's table, his head was down on his desk, and he was crying. I bent low over him and whispered in his ear, "Andre, what's wrong?"

"I miss my daddy," he said.

Andre's father lived in Delaware. When Andre was one, his mother sent him to Delaware to visit. That was the last time Andre had seen his dad. The way Mona told the story—a story Andre made her tell again and again—Andre came home from Delaware so fat that she didn't recognize him when he was brought off the plane. Andre hadn't heard from his father since.

"Do you want to come to the back of the room and talk to me about it, Andre?" I asked. He nodded.

I had seen Andre cry before, but I had never seen him cry

so hard. Tears were streaming down his face. He couldn't catch his breath. I asked him if he thought writing about his feelings might help and he said yes. I gave him a piece of green construction paper, and he started to write. I continued walking around the room and helping other students.

Ten minutes later, I visited Andre at the back table. He was still writing. "Do you want to read what I wrote, Ms. Sentilles?" he asked me. Andre had written a letter to his father asking him to call or write. He told his father he loved him, that he was praying for him, and that he knew God was watching over him. I looked at Andre. He was still crying. I sat down in a chair next to him and opened my arms to hug him. He stood up and sat in my lap. I never wanted to let him go.

When I first met Mona Asher, she was studying to be a beautician. While she was in school, she made money to support her family—Andre and his sister, Dalila—by cleaning people's houses; she called it "doing rooms." She measured her income by rooms. She would say things like, "When I do a few more rooms we can buy his school pictures." Every time I saw her, she had a new hairstyle and seemed very tired.

In the fall, I sometimes watched Andre play football after school. Mona and I would talk on the sidelines. During one of our conversations, I found out about her life and her family. She didn't know her own father. Her mother, sister, and brother were in jail. The two men who were the fathers of her two children were in and out of jail.

"How did you do it, Mona?" I asked, astonished.

"What do you mean, baby?"

"How did you manage to get where you are while everyone around you was going to jail?"

"Simple. While they were going out the back door, I just walked out the front. We stayed out of each other's way. I knew what I wanted, and there wasn't anyone who was going to stop me."

I admired Mona. I loved her. And I loved her even more because she loved Andre so much. But when I was with Mona, I remembered how much of an outsider I was in Compton. Sometimes I felt guilty when we were together. Here I was, a temporary figure in her child's life, driving a Jeep my parents had paid for, taking care of only myself with a teacher's salary, while she struggled to take care of two children and work her way through school. How could I complain about how tired I was, or how stressed my job made me, or how much I missed my family? How could I cry about the pain I saw in Compton, the broken school I taught in? It was her pain. It was her son's school.

One day Andre came to school and told me Mona was sick. An ambulance had taken her to the hospital the night before because she had horrible stomach pains. She had come home that morning. I told Andre I would visit her after school.

At the end of the school day, my friend Jamie Jones drove me to the nursery to buy a plant for Mona, and then she dropped me off at Andre's house. Jamie was taking one of her third grade students to the library. After they were finished there, she would pick me up.

I worked in Compton, but I wasn't familiar with it. I had a false sense of security; I felt safe. I knew my students. I knew where they lived. I knew the neighborhood around my school. I watched my kids walk home every day after school. I waved at them playing in their front yards after school when I drove down their streets. So it never entered my mind that I might not be safe there. I wanted to be safe there. My students lived in Compton, so why shouldn't I work in Compton? Why shouldn't I visit the homes they slept in every single night? Because many students didn't have phones, visiting their homes was sometimes the only way to contact a parent or guardian.

Compton is an unpredictable city. The streets on which children ride bikes one minute become the site of a drive-by shooting the next. But I walked up the Ashers' driveway feeling perfectly safe. They lived in a duplex. The building was an orange-pink color. All the doors and windows were covered with grates and bars. I waved at another student across the street whom I recognized from Garvey.

The minute I walked through the door, I knew something was wrong. A man I had not seen before was sitting on the couch next to Mona. They were engaged in a tense conversation. Mona turned to face me.

"Hey, baby," she said to me.

"How are you feeling?" I asked.

"Better, better. The doctor says it's nerves. This man here stresses me out," she said as she gestured toward the man.

I had walked into the middle of an argument. He was, I found out later, David, Dalila's father. Dalila, eleven years old, was Mona's older child. David had just gotten out of jail and had called Mona the night before to say that he was coming to see her. The thought of seeing him again had made Mona so nervous and afraid that she had been doubled over with abdominal pain. Mona and David were still married. I didn't learn any of this until much later.

While Mona was talking to me, David kept trying to talk to me, too. He stood very close to me. He was barefoot and unshaven. His eyes were bloodshot. I couldn't understand what he was trying to say. I caught bits and pieces: "You know what I'm saying . . . this here woman . . . you know what I'm saying . . . you think she's so nice . . . all her friends say she's so nice . . . she's not nice to me . . . you know . . . I don't see it . . . you see . . . I don't see what they're talking about . . ."

I could tell he was angry—at Mona and at me, this random white woman who showed up at their house and interrupted their discussion. He couldn't stand Mona paying attention to anyone but him. He got mad when she talked to me. He got mad when she talked to Andre or Dalila.

When I didn't give David the response he wanted, he stopped talking to me and started talking to Mona. He asked her for the keys to her car. I took the opportunity to get out of the situation, and I started talking to Andre. I asked him to give me a tour of his house. I had been to his house before, but I had never seen his bedroom.

"Show me where you sleep, Andre," I said.

"OK, Ms. Sentilles," he said, taking my hand and leading me to his bedroom. "This is where me and Dalila sleep." I looked in. Clothing covered the floor. I couldn't see the carpet. Among the clothes were two bare mattresses—no sheets, no blankets, no pillows.

"This is where you sleep?"

"Yeah. It's kind of messy. Want to see my mom's room?" He led me to the door next to his. He couldn't even get her door opened all the way because there was so much stuff in the room: boxes, clothes, papers, a mattress.

When my students walked in the classroom door, I didn't change my expectations for them just because of their situations at home. I expected them all to turn in homework every day. I expected their work to be neat and clean. I expected them to be awake and ready to learn. I believed students meet the level of expectations set for them. The behavior of some students reminded me that they did not come from stable homes. Some slept through school because the noise on their streets or in their living rooms had kept them awake the night before. Others came to school in tears, holding their stomachs because they were so hungry. Still others came to school dirty, hair uncombed, faces unwashed.

Andre, however, came to school every day in beautiful clothes, with perfect homework in his pocket and a smile spread across his face. How he managed to look and act so together I don't know. How Mona managed to maintain a sense of sanity in the middle of her chaotic home, how she managed to bring fruit punch whenever we had a classroom celebration, how she managed to drive to and attend every one of his football games, I don't know. She was a strong woman with a clear sense of what she wanted. She believed in God. She believed in her kids. And she believed in education.

While Andre was giving me the tour, I could hear the argument in the living room escalating. David wanted Mona's car keys, and she wouldn't give them to him. Mona called to me, "Come talk to me, Sarah." I walked with Andre to the living room and sat down on the couch. David got up and went to the kitchen, shouting. Mona continued to talk to me in a calm voice. Her quiet words—which I can't remember at all—were punctuated by shouts from the kitchen: "Bitch . . . damn whore . . . stupid bitch . . ." He opened and closed drawers. He slammed cupboards. I thought I was going to die. I thought he was look-ing for a gun or a knife and was going to kill us all.

During all of this, Dalila sat at the kitchen table and worked on her homework. She was in fifth grade, and she was studying fractions.

Then there was a knock on the door. It was Jamie. An-dre let her in, and as she came into the house, David walked out. Jamie sat at the kitchen table with Dalila and helped her with her homework, adding fractions and finding a common denominator.

I don't remember how we left. Somehow we said good-bye, hugged everyone, made it out the front door, and got into Jamie's car. Once I was inside the car, I was no longer afraid for myself, but for Andre, Mona, and Dalila. I felt guilty. I felt help-less. When Jamie and I got to the corner of their street, I made her turn the car around and drive back to the Ashers' house. I ran inside and gave Mona my phone number and told her to call me if she needed anything. I told her she and her family could sleep at my house if they needed a safe place to stay.

I asked her if she thought she was in physical danger. She said she was fine and that David had never hurt her.

Mona has a huge scar, at least six inches long, on her right arm. I found out later that the last time David was home they had also had an argument, during which he had cut her arm.

I went back to the car, and Jamie drove to the corner again. While we were waiting at the stoplight, Andre rode up to the car on his bike. He talked to us about David and how much he didn't like him. I told Andre I loved him and that I would see him the next day at school.

Andre didn't come to school the next day. Neither did Dalila. Mona didn't answer the phone.

Andre didn't come to school the day after that, either. I was frantic.

Mona brought Andre to school two days after my visit to her house. She looked exhausted. So did Andre. Mona told me what had happened. After I left, David continued to try to take her keys. Mona refused to give them to him, so he hit her. She tried to get away and he chased her. She told Andre and Dalila to run to the neighbors' house.

Andre interrupted Mona to tell me what David had said. "He told me, 'I'm gonna kill your mama! I'm gonna kill your mama!' I shouted at him, Ms. Sentilles. I shouted, 'Don't kill my mama! You can't kill my mama! You're gonna have to hurt me first!' But he just kept chasing my mama and I had to go to the neighbors' house."

Andre was seven years old when he stood on the street in front of his house and shouted at a man who was threatening to kill his mother. I can see Andre standing there, crying, yelling at a man four times his size, a man who wants to kill his mother and steal her car.

Mona ran for her life as this man chased her. She stopped at a pay phone and called 9-1-1. Somehow she found Dalila, who was riding her bike up and down streets looking for her mother, got Andre from the neighbors' house, put everyone in her car, and drove away. "We were on the run for two days," Mona said. "It took the cops two days to come get him. We had to surprise him in the middle of the night. It took them two days. He was on parole and everything. I don't know why they wouldn't help us. So we just had to keep moving, keep driving around. He's in jail now."

During the summer, I took Andre and Bobby, another student from my second grade class, to Venice Beach. We walked along the boardwalk and the two boys pointed out paintings they thought looked like Picasso's. One artist was so impressed with their knowledge that he gave Andre and Bobby a painting of Venice Beach. Then we walked in the sand to the sea. When we got to the edge of the water, Andre took off his shoes and began to run. He ran up and down the beach, arms out like he was flying. He did cartwheels. He did back handsprings. He ran into the water and got his shorts wet. He laughed and laughed.

Like Andre and Bobby, Rosalind Ramon also loved to paint. She wrote a letter to President Clinton asking him to send our class some paint so she could paint like Picasso. She wanted to be an artist when she grew up. In my class, she loved to create what she called "Picasso portraits," portraits with parts of the face mixed up—the ear where the eye should have been, the nose where the mouth should be.

One Saturday, I took five of my students—Rosalind, Ruben, Lorena, Andre, and Eleana—to the Los Angeles County Museum of Art. I met the students in front of Garvey Elementary School at 10:00 on Saturday morning. Rosalind was standing at the gate holding her mother's hand. Her straight brown hair was cut short, to her chin, and she was wearing white shorts, a white shirt, and an oversized denim hat. The six of us piled into my car and began the drive from Compton to the museum.

My five students had never been in a car on the highway before. I was driving west on the highway called the 105 in the carpool lane. At the point where the 105 and another highway, the 110, meet, the carpool lane rises high above the interchange. It looks and feels like a roller coaster. When we reached the interchange, I said, "OK, here we go. Look around and see what you can see."

At the same time, they all started shouting and screaming and waving their hands in the air as if they were on a ride at the fair. Everyone except Rosalind. I could see her in my rearview mirror. Her eyes were squeezed shut and she was grabbing onto her friend Lorena, who was sitting next to her.

"Rosalind, are you OK?" I asked.

"I'm scared, Ms. Sentilles," she said, laughing. "Just tell me when it's over."

At the museum we were stopped by a guard before we reached the ticket counter. "Excuse me," he said, "But I think you are in the wrong place."

I could tell by his tone that he thought we didn't belong at a museum.

"Really?" I said. "Where do you think we should be?"

"Aren't you looking for the Page Museum next door?"

The Page Museum was a natural history museum down the street. "Well, let's see," I said. "Let me ask my students what they came here to see."

"I want to see some cubist paintings by Picasso," Andre said.

"Me, too," echoed Eleana.

"I would like to see some surrealist paintings, please," Ruben said.

"I really like Matisse," Lorena said.

Rosalind stepped up to the front of the group. "I like everything," she said. "But my favorite, I think, is Picasso. Oh, and anything you might have by Salvador Dalí."

The guard looked stunned. "Uh, I guess you are in the right place."

"Yeah," I said, "we are definitely in the right place."

Rosalind winked at me and squeezed my hand.

Feeling like you belong can be a miraculous thing. I put Bobby Randall in the reading group with the best readers even though he couldn't, at first, read very well. In Compton, we were required to group our students by ability during language arts time. My students knew they were being tracked. It doesn't matter if you label the groups with different flowers or colors or cartoon characters, students know which group is the best and which is the worst. When I called Bobby's name to be in the "yellow" group, he didn't hear me. Eleana Dominguez was the best reader in the class, and once he heard she was in the yellow group, I think he tuned out, knowing there was no way he could be in that group, too. I called his name a second time. When he finally heard his name, he came to get his yellow folder from me, slowly, looking at me like I might realize who he was and change his group at any minute. I handed him his folder, touched him on the shoulder, and said, "You can do it, Bobby."

From that moment, Bobby designated himself my personal protector. I have a photograph hanging in my kitchen that was taken by a friend of mine one morning when my class was lining up to come into the classroom. I look completely annoyed. I have one hand on my hip, my eyebrows are furrowed, and I am staring at a student who is outside the frame of the photograph. There are seven students standing around me. Six of them look like they aren't quite awake. Bobby, standing right next to me, has turned around to look at whichever student is giving me a hard time. His whole facial expression seems to say, "What in the world are you doing bothering my teacher?" He looks like he just can't believe someone would not do exactly what I asked him or her to do. He looks personally insulted.

Sometimes when I was teaching, I would get so frustrated I would crouch down on the floor with my knees bent and my hands on my temples. It seemed, somehow, quieter down there. Bobby—ever aware of exactly what I was doing—would then say, "Look at what you all are doing to the teacher. You're giving her a headache. Come on now. Let's keep it down." One of the funniest—and sometimes most frightening—parts of being a teacher was hearing my students say things to each other that I said to them. Hearing my own phrasing and intonation come out of six- and seven-year-old mouths made me giggle. I would circle around the room during language arts centers and hear one student say to another, "Do you think that is a helpful thing to do? Are you participating in a way that is good for the group?"

At the end of every school day, Bobby walked out through the gate of the school with the rest of the students, walked home with his oldest sister, changed into shorts and a T-shirt, and then walked back to school to help me in my classroom. Sometimes he organized papers, other times he asked for extra homework or worked on an art project or read the books in our classroom's library. When I was ready to go, he would gather up some extra paper or crayons to take with him, and I would drive him home. Sometimes I walked into his house with him to check in with his mother. The television was always on, usually tuned to MTV, and three children under the age of two and in diapers would be dancing in front of the television set. Bobby's mother was always working around the house—sweeping, cooking, folding laundry, mopping the kitchen floor. She would stop and talk with me, asking me how Bobby was doing in school. "Your son is very smart," I always told her. Each time she seemed surprised. A small smile would sneak into her tired face, and she would say, "He really is? I knew he was." Bobby's first grade teacher had often told Bobby and his mother that he was a terrible student, a slow reader, and a behavior problem. This teacher was rumored to have made students kneel on broomsticks. If we ever passed her in the hallway, Bobby's whole body would stiffen, and he would walk as far away from her as he could. Sometimes he would even hold my hand.

I had arranged one Saturday to take Bobby and another student to the beach and then to see the movie *Space Jams*. I was to pick him up at his house at 2:00 in the afternoon. My phone woke me at 6:00 in the morning. It was Bobby. "I'm ready," he said.

At the end of that school year, which was my last in Compton, I worked in my classroom for a week, packing and cleaning. Bobby came to school to help me every single day. When we were cleaning out one of the cupboards in my room, we found a big bottle of bubbles and two bubble wands. We went outside, poured the mixture into a Frisbee, and dipped our wands into the bubbles. At the same time, we spun in circles, holding our wands and filling the air with big bubbles. We dipped our wands again and again until we had to sit down on the ground—laughing, surrounded by bubbles.

TAUGHT BY AMERICA

In *No Future without Forgiveness*, Archbishop Desmond Tutu describes April 27, 1994—the day he could vote for the first time in a democratic election in the land of his birth. He writes,

> It was a mountaintop experience. The black person entered the booth one person and emerged on the other side a new, transfigured person. She entered weighed down by the anguish and burden of oppression, with the memory of being treated like rubbish gnawing away at her vitals like some corrosive acid. She reappeared someone new, "I am free."... The white person entered the voting booth burdened by the load of guilt for having enjoyed the fruits of oppression and injustice. He emerged as somebody new. He too cried out, "The burden has been lifted from my shoulders, I am free."[5]

I emerged from my experience in Compton as somebody new. I went to Compton to teach, and I did, but I learned more than I could have ever imagined.

At the end of my second year of teaching, I packed up everything in my classroom, loaded box after box into the back of my car, and drove home to my apartment in Venice. I was done—but somehow I felt like I had just begun.

From the very first moment I stepped into a classroom in Compton, I knew something was required of me, some kind of radical change, but I didn't yet know what. I started small. At the end of my first week of teaching, I marched into a salon and demanded that the stylist change my hair. She answered my urgency with gentleness. "About three inches off?" she asked, holding my long blond hair in her hands.

"No," I said, pointing to my chin. "Cut it to here."

Such outward and visible change was easy. The life change —political, philosophical, emotional—was much more difficult to effect. When our old ways of understanding the world do not work any more, what do we do?

In the middle of my first year of teaching, I knew that a doctorate in comparative literature was no longer the next thing for me. That had been my original plan: teach, apply to graduate school, get on with the rest of my life. I neglected to tell my parents about my change in plan, and so during my second year of teaching, around the time graduate school applications were due, they called several times to check in with me about the applications they imagined I was busy filling out. I tried to explain that I had no idea what I would do when I finished teaching. I am tired, I kept telling them. I am so tired. I don't think they understood how radically my self-understanding had shifted until they called me one night in February. I was sitting on the living room floor with my roommate, Yuki. She was helping me glue my students' artwork on big pieces of butcher paper.

The principal had asked me to create an exhibit for Black History Month. While I was talking to my parents on the phone, I smelled something burning.

"Oh, shit!" I shouted. I had done a lesson that afternoon with my students on measurement. We measured flour and sugar and chocolate chips and made cookie batter. I was baking the cookies to bring to school the following day. "Oh, shit! Oh, shit! The cookies are burned!" And then I started screaming into the phone every single bad word I knew. I told my parents all the things I had kept hidden—I told them about the drive-by shooting I had witnessed, I told them about getting caught in a domestic violence situation, I told them stories of rape and gunshots and burns. And then I started crying and screaming over and over, "I didn't know, I didn't know, I didn't know!" I couldn't stop. They flew me home the next day. I stayed in Texas for a week. They never mentioned graduate school again.

If not graduate school in comparative literature, then what? I had no idea what I was going to do, but I needed money and that meant a job. In March, I applied for a teaching position at the private school in Dallas I attended for first through twelfth grade. I cried when they showed me the supply closet filled with butcher paper, pencils, paper, pens, and highlighters. Stories about teaching in Compton spilled out of me during my interview. The woman who interviewed me, the head of the middle school, wrote me a generous personal check for my classroom. "Buy some books," she said. "And then maybe buy each of your students some ice cream."

On the plane ride back to Los Angeles I screamed at the

man sitting next to me. He had tried to engage me in a conversation about welfare reform. I felt my face get hot. I heard my voice rise.

"Don't take it so personally," he said.

"It is personal!" I shouted. "It *is* fucking personal. These are my kids you are talking about."

The flight attendant nervously moved toward our row. "Is everything OK?" she asked.

"No," I said. "No, it's not."

I knew I was not ready to teach again. Although I had no other prospects, I turned down the job offer from my school in Dallas. Somewhere deep in my being, I knew I needed to write. I knew I had to put on paper the stories swirling in my head. I spent my days working the early morning shift in a neighborhood café and writing in the afternoon. I wrote for a year.

In the middle of that year of writing, I decided I wanted to be ordained as an Episcopal priest. I went to visit Tim Safford, a priest at All Saints.

"I think I want to become a priest," I said.

"Well," he said, looking at me thoughtfully. "I think you should lie down on the floor and see if that feeling will go away."

I did what he said, several times, but the feeling, largely shaped by my experience at All Saints, did not go away. I was convinced that churches, at their best, could be agents of transformation in the world. I thought churches could help people find ways of understanding God that encouraged them to participate in bringing into being a different kind of world. I thought churches could help people resist fear and greed and deep sadness. And so I applied to divinity school, and when I was accepted, I chose Harvard.

In July, I cleaned out my apartment and drove across the country from Los Angeles to Boston. In the parking lot of a hotel in Albuquerque, New Mexico, my car was broken into. They smashed my car's side window and took everything, including my computer, my back-up disks, and my paper copies of the manuscript for this book. I stood at the car, staring at the broken glass scattered on the hotel's parking lot, and screamed.

"You have insurance, ma'am," the police officer said, trying to calm me down.

"They took my book," I said.

"I'm sure you can buy another copy at a bookstore," he said.

When I arrived at divinity school, I was filled with rage. I had several meetings with Dudley Rose, the director of Harvard's field education program. He had a gurgling fountain of water in his office; it soothed me.

"Where is God?" I asked him again and again. "Where is God in all this?"

"Where do you think God is?" he always asked me right back.

At the end of my three years in divinity school, I still thought I wanted to be ordained as an Episcopal priest. I got a job as the director of education at an Episcopal church in a suburb of Boston. I officially entered the ordination process. I met regularly with a small discernment group at the church whose job was to determine whether I was called to ordained ministry. In the middle of the process, the committee found itself in a heated argument over whether it was acceptable for me to live with my boyfriend. This was not how I wanted to spend my time or my energy. I withdrew from the process, and decided, after watching so many of my women friends struggle in the institutional church, that ordained ministry was not for me. At least not yet.

       ◈ ◈ ◈

I left Compton seven years ago. I stopped teaching in 1997 and have rarely been back since. I've been writing *about* my students for seven years, but I haven't written *to* any of them. One day my editor called and suggested that it might be a good idea for me to try to find some of my old students. I hung up the phone and cried, and then I made my plane reservations.

My students are now in ninth grade, much older than when I knew them, but not yet old enough to be listed in telephone directories. Many live with parents or grandparents with different last names. Some are in foster care. Most of the schools don't have websites, and if they do, they haven't been updated in a long time. I found no athletic records, school play programs, school newspaper articles. Nothing.

I felt like I was chasing ghosts.

I decided to call the Teach for America office in Los Angeles. I simply told the nice woman I spoke with that I was writing a book and trying to find my students, and asked for the names and numbers of TFA teachers working at high schools in Compton. She gave me, with no further questioning, the information I requested. I'm not sure she even wrote down my name.

I called all the TFA teachers whose numbers I had been given. Some never called me back. Others let me read them my list of students over the phone.

"Eleana Dominguez?"

"No."

"Dante Rogers?"

"No."

"Taniqua Cameron?"

"Um, yeah, I think she was on my class list at the beginning of the year, but she never showed up."

"Maria Garcia?"

"No."

"Julio Gutierrez?"

"Yes! He was in one of my classes, but he left in December."

"How is he?"

"What do you mean?"

"How is he? What was he like in your class? Did he seem happy?"

"He was a really good student."

While I was speaking to the first teacher, I started to sweat. I hung up the phone and looked at myself in the mirror. My face was completely flushed, my shirt soaked. The thousands of miles of telephone lines stretching from my living room in Cambridge, Massachusetts, into the living room of a teacher in Compton, California, felt more like a few feet, as if we were playing telephone, standing in the same house holding on to cans connected by string. Talking to her, I felt like I was talking to myself seven years ago. She sounded so tired, so frustrated. She told me she had applied to TFA after finishing a master's degree. She requested that she be placed in San Francisco to teach elementary school. TFA placed her, instead, in a Compton high school. She had decided not to finish her two-year commitment with TFA. "I love the kids," she told me, "but I can't handle this. I get death threats, and no one will help me."

None of the TFA teachers I reached had any of my students in their classes currently. I decided to start calling the high schools directly. Compton Unified School District has three high schools: Dominguez, Compton, and Centennial. Centennial lost its accreditation in 2002. As I called the high schools to search for my students, I could feel walls going up everywhere, keeping me out, reminding me I was the outsider.

One guidance counselor, Mrs. Brown, told me I could send her a list of the students I was looking for. "Fax it to me," she said, "and I will see which students go here, and I will call their parents."

Someone was willing to help me. I started to feel afraid. "Do you think they'll want to see me?" I asked her.

"Oh, honey," she said, in the sweetest, warmest voice. "Of course they will want to see you." I started to cry. I wondered how often people came looking for children in Compton.

I called Mrs. Brown two days after I sent her the fax.

"Hi, Mrs. Brown, this is Sarah Sentilles again."

"Uh-huh," she said, as if she had no idea who I was.

"Well, um, I was just calling to see if you have received the fax I sent you."

She told me they didn't have a fax machine in the office. She wouldn't get the fax until the end of the week.

Frustrated, I simply started calling Information.

"City and state?"

"Compton, California."

"Listing?"

I started reeling off all the names I could remember. I knew most parents only by their last names, so I just started asking for them: Roberts, Davis, Garcia. I had no street names, no first names. How many Dominguezes might there be in Compton? How many Rogerses?

Sometimes the operator would tell me she had twenty listings for that last name. Other times she would tell me to "please hold for the number." My stomach would lurch, and then the recorded voice would say, "At the customer's request, this number is unlisted."

I kept trying. And then, finally, I found one.

"Maya Lively," I said to the operator.

"Please hold for the number."

I couldn't believe it. I now had the phone number for Tony Raymond's grandmother. Tony had been one of my favorite first grade students. I picked up the telephone, dialed the number, and a woman answered the phone.

"May I please speak to Maya Lively?" I asked.

"This is she."

"Hi, this is Sarah Sentilles. I was Tony's first grade teacher."

"Oh, Sarah!" I could hear the recognition in her voice. She remembered me. I felt like I had just walked Tony out to her station wagon yesterday. But it wasn't just yesterday. Tony is not in first grade anymore. He's in ninth grade.

"How is Tony?" I asked.

"He's struggling. Having a hard time. You know how the district was when you were here. It hasn't gotten any better. He hasn't connected with a lot of teachers the way he connected with you. He's hanging in there, but it's a struggle."

Hearing her say he had not connected with any teachers the way he connected with me made me feel good and terrible at the same time. All this time. All this time struggling.

"It's good to hear from you," she said. "Tony's been falling in with the wrong people. He's a good kid, you know. The adults he had around him when he was young are not his fault."

"I remember him as a first grader. I remember his smile."

She laughed. "You might not recognize him now. He's growing his hair and hasn't cut it in a while. He wears it in a ponytail. He's thinking of donating his hair to that program for people who have cancer."

"Does he still like to draw?" I asked. When Tony was in first grade, he loved to draw. When he would get upset, I would let him sit at a desk by himself and draw. He could draw for hours.

"Sometimes," she said. "But not much—although he did help his sister with a school project, a family tree. He designed the tree, and he seemed to like doing that."

I will bring him a sketchbook, I thought. A sketchbook and some pencils.

I told her how much Tony had been on my mind, in my heart. She said maybe talking to me was just what he needed. To remember.

"Call us when you get here," she told me. "Just call us and come on by."

I hung up the phone. I stared at the receiver in disbelief. All the doubts I had been pushing down, deep down, for years started to surface. My mind started reeling. Have I been running away? Hiding? Have I been doing what was expected of me because people told me I was good at it? For the last seven years I have been in graduate school studying feminist theology. I struggle daily as a woman and as a feminist in the academy and in the church, but did I simply find a new struggle that was hard, but not so complicated? The struggle now is mine—I struggle against sexism and misogyny, and, even if I'm the only one, I get to think I'm right. In Compton, I was part of the problem. My whiteness. My class. My privilege. I was the one being struggled against, and I struggled with myself.

I knew returning to Compton was the right thing to do, but I was terrified. Those days walking out to the car to tell Mrs. Lively how Tony's day had been, the day she told me he had a good day because he really liked wearing his tennis shoes, were so fresh in my mind. But seven years had passed. It had taken me that long to heal, to recover—seven years to be able to even think about going back, to be able to want to find the children I knew, to risk finding them, to risk feeling all those feelings again, to risk remembering children running to me, surrounding me, to risk feeling like something was demanded of me, but not knowing what it was, or if I could do it.

After I left, Compton felt like another world to me. But Compton is *not* another world, it's just another city. All I had to do was get on an airplane and fly to Los Angeles and then rent a car to drive to Compton. Then I would see Tony. He had spent seven more years in the Compton school system, and I had been at Harvard, complaining. I felt ashamed. Suddenly I knew I was accountable to Tony—not to my parents, or to my academic advisor, but to Tony, a boy I knew when he was six years old. I stand in judgment of myself imagining him standing in judgment of me.

I want to know these children again. Not the small ones I carry around in my head, not the remembered children, but the real, alive, struggling, brilliant, complicated ones they are now. I want to be relevant. I want, someday, to be able to stand in front of Tony and say, yes, yes, yes, I let you change my life. Look what it has become.

My partner, Eric Toshalis, flew with me to Los Angeles. When we arrived in Compton, I wanted to go immediately to my first elementary school, Madison. We parked on the street across from the school.

"Take a deep breath," Eric said. "Now, remember what we talked about. No crying until the end of the day. When we get back to the hotel you can cry as much as you want to." He turned to look at the front of the school. "Wow," he said.

"Pretty run-down," I said.

"That's not what I meant. I was looking at the roses." At Madison, the tiny strip of grass in front of the school is lined with rosebushes. Roses bloom all over Compton, practically year round, covering fences, front porches, yards. The sweet smell of roses sometimes fills the air when the wind is right.

We walked past two signs on our way to the office. One read "Knowledge Is the Only Excellence" and the other "We Welcome Parents Here." We walked into the office. It was newly renovated. A huge file cabinet lined the back wall. The top of the cabinet was covered in tiny collectors' statues of white children—white children running, fishing, studying, reading. We signed in, were given name tags, and left the office to begin to walk around the school. Children were everywhere—lining up for lunch, running to recess, following teachers into their classrooms, waiting in the nurse's office. There was not one white child among them.

"They're the same size as I remember them," I said to Eric. I could almost fool myself into thinking my students had not grown. It took some effort for me to remember these were not the same students I had taught. Some of the students I was watching run around now had not even been born when I taught here. I noticed there were new bathrooms and new glass blocks cut into the outside of the classroom walls so you could actually see inside the classrooms. We walked out to the yard. It looked exactly the same—an enormous stretch of dirt, tetherball poles with strings and no tetherballs, virtually no playground equipment. We stood, looking, and then a white man walked up to us and said, "Have you come here to give us new playground equipment?"

I turned to look at him. He was covered in children. They were holding on to his legs, swinging from his arms. "We could sure use some so they stop climbing on me," he said, laughing.

Just looking at us—two blond white people, one of us carrying a clipboard—he knew we didn't belong and assumed we had something to give. He asked us who we were and what we were doing there.

"We're just visiting," I said. "I used to be a teacher here."

"Why did you decide to come back? Are you doing a project or something?" he asked.

"Just curious," I said. I didn't tell him I was writing a book. My omission burned, making me blush. Eric looked sideways at me, and then told him he was a doctoral student at Harvard Graduate School of Education.

"Are you a researcher, too?" he asked Eric, gesturing at my clipboard. I wished I had left it in the car.

Eric nodded. "A researcher and a teacher."

We watched a group of boys running around at the edge of the yard kicking up dirt. "Only two elementary schools in Compton have any grass," he said.

"Is it alright for them to kick around dirt like that?" I asked.

"They're not kicking dirt. They have a ball."

I squinted my eyes to see better. "It's not a ball," I said. "It's a can."

He started talking to us about what it is like to teach at Madison now. "You know," he said, "they want to blame the teachers, but it's not the teachers' fault these kids aren't doing well. It's not the teachers, and it's not poverty."

"Well, what is it, then?" Eric asked.

"They spent the last decade bringing the best minds of the state here, and they still can't figure it out. I did my own survey. You know what? Fifty-three percent of the students here say they hate themselves. Twenty-five percent admit to trying to disrupt their teacher at least twice a week. We're trying to fix this here by changing the environment of the school, by making this a place where the kids want to be."

"Is it working?" I asked.

"Well, we got the kids to say, 'We come here to learn!' every day, and if you ask me, that's a big change."

I could have told him it was not a big change. We chanted that when I taught there. The principal made us line up together on hot black asphalt in the mornings before we went into our classroom and chant inane slogans like that. I used to find it humiliating. It seemed to me the very fact of having to say something like that admitted defeat. I once heard author Jonathan Kozol say that when you make schoolchildren chant a slogan you're already suggesting the opposite is true. Otherwise, why would they have to say it out loud? Isn't it obvious that children come to school to learn?

He turned to leave. As he was walking away, he called over his shoulder to Eric, "Come do your research here. I'll set you up. No one ever comes to do research here. We need you."

We walked to the office to sign out. I bought a yellow Madison Elementary School T-shirt with a picture of a lion on it from the secretary, and then we drove to Garvey Elementary. I barely recognized it. Garvey was obviously one of the two elementary schools in Compton with grass. When I was there, it had a dirt yard. Now the yard was green. It looked almost luscious compared to the dirt and asphalt we found at Madison. The campus was crowded with new portable buildings. One section of the school was being gutted. I couldn't find my way around. I felt disoriented. I walked to the spot where I thought my classroom used to be, and there was nothing there. Diagonally across from me there were several rows of portable buildings that had not been there before. I couldn't discern any order in their placement. They seemed to have been scattered around, like seeds sprinkled from above. One set of new portable buildings was two stories tall.

There were no signs on any of the rooms, but we eventually found our way to the main building and the front office. The same secretary who had been there when I was there was behind the front desk. I told her who I was. She tilted her head and looked at me. She squinted her eyes. "Yeah," she said. "I remember you."

I asked her if my classroom still existed. She said no. And so we left.

We drove around Compton looking for a place to eat lunch. We could find nothing but fast food. There are almost no businesses in Compton other than fast food chains, auto parts stores, a Food Mart, and more liquor stores than we could count. We found a Subway. We ate lunch and then went back to the hotel.

That evening, we drove to Tony's house. Tony and his grandmother were sitting on their front porch waiting for me. They both stood and waved when they saw me. I told Eric to wait in the car. When I got out of the car, Mrs. Lively shouted, "Who's that in the car?"

"My boyfriend, Eric," I said.

"Don't leave him in there. Bring him up with you." I waved at Eric and gestured for him to come inside. We climbed the steps to their second-floor apartment. We stood on a big porch overlooking the whole neighborhood. Mrs. Lively gave me an enthusiastic hug. Then I hugged Tony. When I taught him he was still losing baby teeth. Now, of course, he had all of his teeth, but one of his front top teeth was chipped.

"Nice ponytail," I said. He smiled.

"This is a beautiful porch," I said. The porch wrapped almost all the way around her apartment.

"We've lived here ten years now," she said. "I've wanted to move, to get my kids into another district, but they were moved so much when they were little that they really don't want to move again. I know all my neighbors." She pointed to the house across the street. "They've lived here forty years. The people next door have been here thirty years. Nice people all around here. I had to call the police once, though. Some Spanish gangs started coming in here, selling drugs right in front of the house. I called the police and told them this was not going to work. And they stay away now."

I had brought a photo album with me, a collection of all the photographs I had taken of Tony's class. I asked him if he wanted to see it. He did, so he sat down on a deck chair and opened the book. He turned the pages slowly and carefully. His sister came and stood behind him. He told me some of the students used to go to his church.

Maya Lively is the primary caretaker of her four grandchildren, her mother, and her neighborhood. "I had to stop working in the schools, Sarah," she said. "I would get knots in my stomach at the end of the summer when it was time for school. I knew I would have to go to the schools and fight for basic things for my kids. I would have to fight to get them into different classes with better teachers, fight sometimes just to get them a teacher. One year, they had no classrooms for my kids. The district would do nothing about it. I had to call Child Protective Services to complain. Another year, Tony's sister had a different sub every day for an entire year. Some of the classrooms they put my kids in have forty-three kids in them. So many of them are foster kids, with emotional needs and problems. How in the world are you supposed to handle that as a teacher?"

"I saw some construction going on at a few of the elementary schools," I offered.

"Oh, yeah," she said. "Don't be fooled by that. I saw some construction, too, so I asked the principal how many classrooms were being added. She just said, 'Classrooms? We're expanding the faculty parking lot.' Oh, great, I told her, that will help."

She turned to look at Eric. "Is this your first time in Compton?"

"Yes," he said.

"Have you all driven around much?"

"A little bit," he said.

"I'll tell you what. Drive over the border into the next town, and you'll feel the difference. Go ahead and drive all the way over to Long Beach. Go to the pier and see the way it's been developed. I want to ask our new mayor why we don't have anything like that here in Compton. What's going on?" she asked.

"There are a lot of liquor stores," Eric said. "I haven't seen any bookstores though."

She laughed. "I have to drive thirty minutes to get to the

nearest bookstore." She took a deep breath. She took her glasses off and rubbed her nose. "I'm so tired," she said. "I'm so tired of fighting this district. My blood pressure is up. I almost have ulcers. This is no good for my health."

I had prepared a list of questions for Tony on the plane. I tried to remember them so I wouldn't have to look at my clipboard. Just carrying it still felt funny. "Do you like school, Tony?" I asked.

"Not really," he said.

"Why not?" I asked.

"My teachers don't like me. They don't really know me."

"How can you tell they don't like you?"

"By how they treat me, how they tell me what to do, how often they make me move my seat."

"What else do you not like about school?" I asked.

"The teachers don't explain things. They just give us work."

"Do you still like to draw?" I asked.

"Not much," he said.

"You used to love it, at least that's what I remember," I said. He smiled shyly.

"I brought you a sketchbook and some pencils. If you don't want to draw with them, you can just use it as a notebook." When I handed him the sketchbook, Tony's smile got bigger. He ran his hands over the cover of the book. He didn't let go of it the whole time we were there.

Tony's sister kept coming out onto the porch to show Mrs. Lively her homework. She would hand Mrs. Lively a piece of notebook paper. Mrs. Lively would stop talking for a minute, look at her work, and then say something like, "Don't you need one more paragraph here?" Then Tony's sister would go back into the house and smile at Tony through the window. They smiled at each other a lot.

I asked Tony several more questions about school, and he answered all of them with short answers. The only question Tony asked me was about this book. "What's your book about?" he asked.

"It's about you. It's about all the students I got to know while I was teaching here."

"Oh," he said.

"Is that alright with you?" I asked.

"Yeah," he said.

"I'll send it to you," I said.

"He's so excited about the book," Mrs. Lively said. "He's been talking about it since you told me about it on the phone."

"I can send you a copy of the chapter about Tony before it's published," I said.

"Don't worry," she said. "We trust you."

Eric took photographs of us, we exchanged addresses, and then we said good-bye. Eric and I walked down the steps toward the courtyard of the building. Underneath the porch, just out of Mrs. Lively's line of vision, four kids were drinking beer. We kept turning around and waving.

The next morning, I visited Centennial High School. When Eric and I walked in, the first thing we saw was a giant red mural of a face of a Native American, complete with stereotypical face paint and feathers. The school mascot is an Apache, and almost every mural around the school has something to do with "war cries." An African American woman sat at the front desk, joking with a police officer and a few students. She periodically interrupted her conversation to yell at someone in the hallway to get back to class. We walked up to her desk.

"Can I help you?" she asked.

"Yes, please. We are here to see Mr. Figueroa." He was a guidance counselor I had spoken with on the phone.

"What room is he in?"

"I don't know," I said. I felt like I seemed suspicious.

"OK. Let me see." She looked through a binder listing the teachers and their classroom numbers. "Room 38. Please sign in here and fill out these name tags."

"Thank you," I said. I signed us in and wrote our names on name tags. We turned to walk away, and then the woman at the desk shouted, "Sarah! Come back here!"

I turned around.

"Are you both named Sarah?" she asked.

"Um, no," I said.

"Well then, you signed yourself in twice, and if there's a fire we'll be running around looking for two Sarahs." I had been so nervous when I signed the book that I wrote my name twice instead of writing Eric's name.

"Sorry about that."

She pointed us in the direction of Mr. Figueroa's room. We passed boys playing basketball, girls hanging out on picnic tables, couples making out against walls, and rows and rows of seemingly jumbled portable buildings. We walked into Mr. Figueroa's office and waited while he talked with several students at his desk. His office was a tiny cubicle among several cubicles crammed inside a portable building. When he was free, he motioned for us to come sit at his desk, a large brown one that barely fit inside the cubicle. I explained what I was doing, and I asked him if he could help me find out if any of my old students were at Centennial.

"I could," he said, "but our computer system is down. It has been down for three weeks."

"Wow," I said. "What are you going to do about graduation and grades and the end of the year?"

He pointed to a huge stack of paper on his desk. "That's what I'm going to do. I have to write everything on paper." The paper was all different colors and sizes. I remember that when I was teaching it was nearly impossible to get white paper. I usually had to use "goldenrod." I still hate that color.

"Come back tomorrow," he said. "Maybe the computer will be working."

I returned the next morning, first thing. I asked Eric to wait in the car. I signed in at the desk, and then I found Mr. Figueroa. "OK," he said. "Tell me again what you are doing." I told him about the book. He took a deep breath. "I'm going to have to take you up to the office. The computers are still down, but the principal has one that works."

I'm not sure if he was telling me the truth, or if this was his way of getting me to ask the principal for permission. I imagine he felt like he was doing something wrong just talking to me, and I don't blame him.

We walked across the campus. It felt like a maze. We passed a small white tent. A few security guards were gathered underneath it to stay out of the sun. We reached the principal's office. It seemed to have been recently renovated. It was a huge open space with high ceilings and almost no furniture. Two women sat at randomly placed desks. We walked to the back of the large room where there was a small corner office.

"Excuse me, Dr. Sanchez," he said, knocking gently on the door.

"Yes?"

"Um, this is, um . . ." Mr. Figueroa turned to look at me. "What is your name again?"

"I'm Sarah Sentilles," I said. "I used to be a teacher in Compton, and I'm writing a book about some of the students I used to teach when they were in elementary school, and I'm trying to find them."

The principal looked up from what he was working on at his desk. His eyes were cold. I felt he was glaring at me. "Who sent you here?" he asked.

"Just me," I said.

Then he started firing questions at me. "What is your purpose? Why are you here? Do you have parental permission?"

"Um, no," I said.

"Then the answer is no. I can give you no information." The principal's eyes seemed full of hate as he spoke to me. He turned back to whatever he was doing. My eyes burned with tears. I was sure my face was bright red. I felt like I had been caught in the act of doing something terrible.

"Sorry," Mr. Figueroa whispered to me as he shook my hand.

I turned and left. During my visits to schools in Compton, I had been surprised that so many people let me walk right onto their campuses. All I had to do was sign my name in a book, put on a sticky name tag, and I was free to roam. This principal stopped me. He was protecting his students. What felt so hard to me was that he was protecting his students from me.

"That was quick," Eric said when I climbed back in the car.

"Yeah," I said. "Let's go to Dominguez."

I had an appointment at Dominguez High School, Tony's high school, to meet with Mrs. Jackson, another guidance counselor. I had already faxed her a list of my students. We found the school, but we couldn't find an entrance. We drove around the block three times. The entire school was surrounded by a high fence. "I guess this is a closed campus," Eric said. We finally found a break in the fence, guarded by a man in a security uniform. We were early, so we sat in the parking lot and waited. We could hear a band practicing "Pomp and Circumstance." One boy was playing a drum outside on the grass. He was really good.

When it was time for my appointment, I got out of the car and walked toward what I thought was the front office, but it was a bathroom. I asked a group of girls to point me toward the counselors' offices. I walked through a courtyard and then passed lines and lines of portable buildings with black numbers stenciled on the doors. Most of the doors were propped open, trying to get some fresh air into the buildings on such a hot day. After walking into two portable buildings that were not counselors' offices, I finally found Mrs. Jackson.

I sat down across the desk from her.

"So," she said, "what have you been doing since you left Compton?"

"I have been in graduate school."

"All this time? You must be getting a Ph.D. What are you studying?"

"Religion."

"What kind of religion?"

"Theology," I said. "Feminist and liberation theology." I began to talk a little bit about my plans to write a dissertation on critical imagination. She looked at me strangely, so I stopped.

"Do you believe in God?" she asked.

I knew the question required a strategic answer. "Yes," I said. "Yes, I do."

My answer seemed to relax her. "So now you're writing a book about your students," she said.

"Yes," I said.

"With their permission, I assume," she said. I wanted to crawl under the table. "Three of your students go to this high school."

I told her I knew Tony Raymond was one of the three students here who used to be mine because I had spent some time with him and his grandmother yesterday. This seemed to lend me some legitimacy in her eyes.

"Who are the other two students?" I asked.

"Prince Stephens and Dante Rogers," she said. She called their parents to ask if they would give permission for their children to see me. Both parents said yes. Mrs. Jackson then handed a student who was waiting in the office two notes and asked him to deliver them to the boys' classrooms. I sat and waited.

Prince came in first. I stood up. I recognized him, but he

looked really different. The little boy I had taught now looked like a man. He was much taller than me. He wore his hair in braids. Mrs. Jackson walked over to us.

"Do you remember her, Prince?" she asked.

"Yeah," he said. "She was my teacher."

"You all can stay in here and catch up," she said, "or you can walk around."

"What would you like to do, Prince?" I asked.

He just shrugged.

"What were you doing in class?" I asked.

"Sleeping."

"Why?"

"I finished my work."

"What was your work?"

"A word search."

"About what?"

"Airplanes."

"Were you studying airplanes?"

"No, it was in English class."

"So they were just wasting your time?"

"Yeah."

I showed him the photo album I had brought with me, and he seemed to like looking at the photographs. When he got to the photograph of himself working with clay, I asked what he was doing in the picture, and he told me he remembered making a dinosaur. He answered most of my questions with one-word answers. Sometimes I could catch a hint of a smile on his face, but mostly there was a real hardness about him.

"What do you think you would like to do when you finish high school?" I asked.

"I want to be a professional football player."

"Have you been playing football?"

"Yes," Prince said.

"Do you like offense or defense better?"

"Defense."

"Why?" I asked.

"Because I get to hit people," he said. "In offense you get hit; in defense you get to hit."

When Dante walked into the office, I barely recognized him. I had to look hard to find the face of the little boy I used to know. He was huge, fat even. Mrs. Jackson asked him if he remembered me, and he looked at me, looked back at her, and said no.

"No?" she asked.

"No," he said.

"I remember you," I said. "I remember your mother would write you notes and leave them in your lunch bag."

"Can I go back to class?" Dante asked Mrs. Jackson.

"Of course," she said.

"I'm ready, too," Prince said.

"OK," she said.

After the boys left, Mrs. Jackson tried to make me feel better about Dante. "He's living with his grandmother now," she said. "I wanted to ask him what happened with his mother, but I didn't want to embarrass him. He's not my counselee."

"Thank you for all your help," I said.

"I'm impressed you still remember your students and came all the way back here to find them, to try to reconnect."

"It would have been more impressive if I'd stayed," I said.

"Well, I think it's impressive you're here now, even though part of the reason you came back is for research," she said and pointed to my clipboard.

I wanted Compton to be different when I returned. I wanted classrooms to have enough books, teachers to have enough support, students to have enough love and intellectual stimulation and the deep knowledge that they are worth something and this country knows it. Instead, I found a school district very much like the one I had left years ago—overworked teachers, old buildings, broken playground equipment.

This story and these children have stuck with me for seven years. While I taught the seventy-plus students who came through my two classrooms how to read, how to add and subtract and multiply, how to hold a pencil, how to paint like Pablo Picasso, and how to solve word problems, they taught me that my privilege depends on the creation of cities like Compton. That corruption and greed lead to calculated, intentional decisions that leave some children in this country without food and books and others with an abundance of both. That there is joy everywhere. That there is a hope that shimmers and shines in the most difficult spaces. That I am racist, and my country is racist, and the wounds of this racism are still raw. That I am capable of deep love and of being loved. That systemic poverty is violent. That how and what we think matters. That my life could be made new. I will carry these children in my heart forever. They are the lens through which I view the world and make decisions. They are the ones to whom I hold myself accountable.

Throughout my time in Compton, I found it almost incredible that students kept coming back to school. Every morning driving to school, I passed streams of children walking to school, laughing, playing with each other, some even skipping. Watching them, it was possible to imagine that they were heading to a gorgeous campus with classrooms filled with new books and state-of-the-art equipment. They looked so happy, so full of hope. What is it, I wondered, that keeps them coming back?

My students used to ask me to read them the same stories again and again. And even though they knew the endings, they would always get nervous in the middle of the stories when things started heating up. What if she doesn't say the magic spell in time? What if he loses the magic ring this time? What if no one ever finds her? What if he never comes back? What if, what if, what if?

The possibility that things could be different, that things *should* be different, keeps me sorting through these memories, trying to arrange them in a perfect pattern so that some kind of meaning will emerge. I wanted to write a different ending, for me and for my students. I longed for an answer, a solution, a clear direction. But no matter how much I wrote and rewrote, arranged and rearranged, I was left with only fragments—missing teeth and textbooks, bullet holes and gunshots, laughter and light, hunger and abundance, shouting police and screaming children, images of children slapped and children held.

I struggled while I was teaching in Compton. When I

stopped teaching, I struggled harder still. I didn't know what to do with what I had experienced. I asked myself, again and again, "How must my life change in response to what I have witnessed?" My conversion, my awakening to the understanding that I am accountable and responsible for what is happening in Compton and in places like Compton across this country, devastated me. But it also liberated and empowered me. If I am accountable and responsible, then what I do matters. I believe something else is possible for me and for these children. I hope that my life, lived with integrity, lived awake and engaged, lived with these children in my heart and in my mind, will do more good than harm. I don't know what the outcome of my actions will be, but I will keep at it, knowing other people are keeping at it too, and hope that something good and just might emerge. This is faith for me.

ACKNOWLEDGMENTS

This book was a group effort. Thank you to my parents, Ann and Irwin Sentilles, who subsidized my year of writing, lit a fire for justice in the hearts of four children, let their lives be changed by my time in Compton, and continue to help make the kind of life I choose to live possible. Thank you to my siblings, Emily, Irwin, and Della, who are actively engaged in making the world a better place. Thank you to my grandparents, Vera and Irwin Sentilles and Bill and Janet Sherwood. Thank you to the teachers at Greenhill School who taught me how to write: Mr. Degener, Ms. Eastus, Ms. Edwards, Mr. Goodman, Ms. Roman, Dr. Stewart, Ms. Velvin, and Mr. Williams. Thank you to all the people (in addition to my family) who have read this manuscript in one form or another: Pam Bator, Tanya Clement, Lane Dilg, Katie Ford, Claudia Highbaugh, Julie King, Stephanie Paulsell, and Ron Thiemann. Thank you to Gordon Kaufman for helping me claim a different kind of faith. Thank you to Maylen Dominguez Arlen, Phil Arlen, and Yuki Murata, who lived through this time with me and encouraged me to write. I would not be me without you. Thank you to all my friends from Yale who visited my classrooms and listened to the stories from my classrooms—Maylen, Yuki, Chantal Forfota, Abby Greensfelder,

Anne Guerry, Sara Levine, Amy Lief, Vicki Politis, and Annie Staebler. Thank you to my magnificent and wise goddaughter, Sofia Eleana Arlen, for being so full of life in a time that was also full of sorrow. Thank you to my friend Taura Null for swimming in oceans with me and believing in light and words. Thank you to the mad priestesses of the Sahelis—Tovis Page, Laura Tuach, and Ann McClenahan. Thank you to Women-Church at Harvard Divinity School, and to Lynette Banks and Mercer Riis for their encouragement while I struggled through the discernment process. Thank you to Martina Verba, who returned my self to me. Thank you to Amy Walsh, a super-heroine and an artist who knows creativity is essential for justice. Thank you to the man who stole my computer and the manuscript for this book out of my car in Albuquerque, New Mexico. (This book was much better the second time around, and I hope you have found what you were looking for.) Thank you to Rex Dupont and Jonathan Zittrain for loving these stories and helping me get this book published. Thank you to my fabulous agent, Elisabeth Weed, and to Ike Williams. Thank you to Joanne Wyckoff, my incredible editor at Beacon, for her careful and insightful work, and thank you to Brian Halley, Robin DuBlanc, Lisa Sacks, and everyone else at Beacon who worked on this project. Thank you to the Teach for America teachers and the guidance counselors at the high schools in Compton who helped me find these students again. Thank you to Gloria House and Anthony Paschal for welcoming me into their lives and their home. Thank you to Eric Toshalis for loving my biggest self and for being my teacher, my partner, and my love. And, most importantly, thank you to all the students who came through my classrooms. I worry that I got more out of my relationship with you than you did. I worry that I will get more out of this book than you will. I offer these pages to you.

NOTES

1. http://www.comptonpolicegangs.com/compton-history.htm.

2. In 1993, the Compton Unified School District (CUSD) was the first California school district to be taken over by the state. The district, with twenty-nine thousand students and thirty-seven schools, was in trouble. Years of corruption and mismanagement had led to a financial crisis of epic proportions, and the performance of Compton students was among the lowest in the state. In exchange for a bailout loan of 20 million dollars, the Compton School Board handed over their district to the state of California. The Compton School Board was reduced to an advisory panel, and the state-appointed district administrator had full control of CUSD.

3. Ruth L. Ozeki, *My Year of Meats* (New York: Penguin, 1998), 334.

4. http://archive.aclu.org/news/no71097b.html.

5. Desmond Tutu, *No Future without Forgiveness* (New York: Doubleday, 1999), 7–8.